Finding Yourself in Chaos

Finding Yourself in Chaos

Self-Discovery for Religious Leaders in a Time of Transition

James R. Newby and Mark Minear

An Alban Institute Book

ROWMAN & LITTLEFIELD
Lanham • Boulder • New York • London

Published by Rowman & Littlefield
An imprint of The Rowman & Littlefield Publishing Group, Inc.
4501 Forbes Boulevard, Suite 200, Lanham, Maryland 20706
www.rowman.com

86-90 Paul Street, London EC2A 4NE

British Library Cataloguing-in-Publication Information Available

Library of Congress Cataloging-in-Publication Data

Names: Newby, James R., author. | Minear, Mark, 1953- author.
Title: Finding yourself in chaos : self-discovery for religious leaders in a time of transition / James R. Newby and Mark Minear.
Description: Lanham, Maryland : Rowman & Littlefield Publishers, [2022] | Includes bibliographical references and index. | Summary: "This volume guides religious leaders during turbulent life events that challenge their ability to serve as effective ministers. Encouraging careful introspection and a focus on personal fulfillment and self-care, the book challenges all readers to build support systems for themselves and their faith communities"—Provided by publisher.
Identifiers: LCCN 2022021199 (print) | LCCN 2022021200 (ebook) | ISBN 9781538166741 (cloth) | ISBN 9781538166758 (paperback) | ISBN 9781538166765 (ebook)
Subjects: LCSH: Christian leadership. | Change (Psychology)—Religious aspects—Christianity.
Classification: LCC BV652.1 .N4175 2022 (print) | LCC BV652.1 (ebook) | DDC 262/.1—dc23/eng/20220711
LC record available at https://lccn.loc.gov/2022021199
LC ebook record available at https://lccn.loc.gov/2022021200

♾️™ The paper used in this publication meets the minimum requirements of American National Standard for Information Sciences—Permanence of Paper for Printed Library Materials, ANSI/NISO Z39.48-1992.

With gratitude to all the participants in our Sacred Chaos *seminars who shared their stories of pain and hope. We dedicate this book to you.*

~

Contents

~

Acknowledgments

The authors are grateful to many people who have been instrumental in the development of this work. We express our gratitude to Natalie Mandziuk, acquisitions editor at Rowman and Littlefield Publishing Group. She was most encouraging when we first approached her about this project. We are grateful to our families, Elizabeth and Karla, Alicia and David, Andrew and Hilliary, and Emily and Ryan for their patience and loving support as we worked through the months to bring this project to completion. Thank you to Cincinnati Friends Meeting and the Des Moines Pastoral Counseling Center for allowing us the time to write, even while we continued to meet our institutional obligations. Judith Dancy and Joe Rohr were instrumental in writing the journaling and spiritual autobiography parts of the fifth chapter, "Knowing Who You Are." Both Joe and Judith were important participants in the beginning of the NET (Nurturing Experience Theologically) Groups Program (as outlined in the book *Gathering the Seekers*). To them we express our gratitude.

The authors completed this book within the beautiful and spiritual surroundings of the little community called New Harmony, Indiana. This is the community of the Roofless Church, the Red Geranium Restaurant, the Poet's House, and the Tillich garden, where the remains of the famous theologian Paul Tillich are buried. It was also the home of Jane Blaffer Owen, a patron of the arts who over the years generously supported the authors in sponsoring *Sacred Chaos*. Jane has left this earth physically, but in New Harmony her spiritual presence is on every street and in every historic structure. Over the years, we have always returned to New Harmony as a favorite place to retreat, simmer, write, and renew our spiritual energies. We are grateful for the memory of Jane Owen, and for the inspiration that this wonderful little community instills within us.

Finally, we thank all those religious leaders who have participated in our *Sacred Chaos* seminars. Wherever we have gathered across the United States, our groups have been open, vulnerable, and supportive of one another. As we became spiritual friends, we formed beloved and caring communities. For sharing your pain and for your willingness to develop plans of action that would change your life dances, we congratulate you and we thank you. It is to you that we dedicate this book.

~

Introduction

Sacred Chaos: Processing *Pain*, Recovering *Passion*, Experiencing *Journey*

Pain and loss produce chaos. Chaos can have gentle beginnings, such as an inner tug deep within our souls that awakens us to the realization that the life we are now living is not fulfilling. Chaos can also begin in more dramatic ways—the death of a loved one, divorce, the loss of a job, academic failure, or retirement. Whatever the impetus, chaos is uncomfortable. It moves us out of familiar patterns and known ways; it causes us to reevaluate what is important and how our lives are being lived, and, if we heed the signs, it sets us on a journey of seeking more of what is missing. Chaos in our lives and in our ministries also affects the way we lead. Recognizing it in our lives, and dealing with it, will help us prepare for a new chapter in our personal journeys and in our ministries. Ignoring it or self-medicating the chaos we feel will eventually lead to emotional and spiritual problems and a loss of interest and passion in our leadership responsibilities.

For many years, the authors have been co-leaders of a seminar titled *Sacred Chaos: A Seminar for Religious Leaders in Transition*. The main purpose of this seminar is to assist in the spiritual and emotional renewal of religious leaders. It was Ernest Hemingway who wrote in A *Farewell to Arms*, "The world breaks everyone and afterward many are strong at the broken places."[1] To paraphrase Hemingway, the institutional church has broken and will break many religious leaders. Our hope with every *Sacred Chaos* seminar is that we will help religious leaders become strong in their broken places and support them through some of their most difficult life passages, e.g., retirement, divorce, midlife, and in recent times the COVID-19 pandemic, the tribalization of our society and the religious institutions we serve, as well as all the problems associated with the declining influence of religion in our culture. The goals of *Sacred Chaos* are four:

1. To provide a supportive group and safe haven for religious leaders who are confused, in pain, or are questioning their vocation, and a place where they can be authentic and vulnerable.
2. To sensitize religious leaders to the early signs of burnout, and to take proactive and preventive measures to address the painful issues in congregational life and/or in their personal lives.
3. To help religious leaders clarify their call to ministry by supporting them in understanding their lives as a spiritual journey, even as they are experiencing chaos; to counsel them and provide a safe place to discuss their pain, helping them understand their angers and fears and supporting them in the process of recovering their ministerial passion. Or, to help religious leaders realize that there are other possibilities beyond professional ministry where their gifts can be used.
4. To help religious leaders understand how their self-care is directly associated with their effectiveness in caring for others.

Participants in the seminar gather on a Monday afternoon, and the leaders discuss with each person individually why he or she wants to participate in such a seminar. The leaders give each participant a small journal for making notes and for sharing their feelings. Each morning begins with worship based on silence, while one of the seminar facilitators reads an appropriate passage from a text by a religious leader who has experienced chaos in his or her own life and in that vulnerability was able to write about it.

The first day focuses on the topic of processing pain. Participants are asked to self-examine their lives, asking these questions: "What am I feeling?" "At whom am I angry?" "What do I fear?" "How have I been hurt?" "How have I sought to resolve my issues of pain . . . within my family, within my network of friends, within the religious institution I am serving?" "How am I self-medicating my pain?"

The second day focuses on the topic of recovering passion. The first casualty of inner pain is the loss of passion, and 99 percent of the persons attending this seminar have lost their passion in ministry. Again through self-examination, they ask: "How do I define passion?" "How is it experienced?" "What does it feel like when I lose it?" "How can it be recovered?"

The third day centers on the topic of experiencing journey. Focus questions include the following: "What is my story?" "Who are my people: family and faith community?" "How have I experienced God in my spiritual journey?" "When does God feel close?" "Does God feel distant? How so?" What the leaders try to help participants understand is that their lives can be understood as a spiritual pilgrimage, and that there is no wrong journey or right journey, just a *journey*. We encourage seminar participants to ask throughout each experience of life, "How is God working here?" and "What spiritual lessons am I learning?"

In *Sacred Chaos*, many different types of ministers from many denominations are brought together. They begin their time with one another as wounded individuals, and by the end of the week they are a beloved community . . . a community in which they have become vulnerable with one another in processing their pain, recovering their passion, and understanding their journey in life as a spiritual pilgrimage. The title of this volume has a double meaning. These religious leaders find themselves in chaos, but they also *find* themselves in chaos. Chaos does not have to be a negative experience; it can be made sacred if those who find themselves in it are willing to do the work to make it a positive experience of spiritual growth. It can indeed be a journey of self-discovery as we seek to do ministry in this time of transition.

Throughout this volume, the authors will share out of their experience in leading *Sacred Chaos* seminars, as well as expand on their personal experiences as religious leaders. They will also share various profiles of religious leaders and the issues that the participants were willing to share with one another. Of course, names have been changed to ensure confidentiality. It is the hope of the authors that by sharing their experiences and the issues they encountered in *Sacred Chaos*, those in religious leadership today and those studying to become the religious leaders of tomorrow will learn from the signposts that those who have experienced chaos have left us. Although each religious leader is unique and seeks to "follow the grain in your own wood," to borrow a phrase from Howard Thurman, there are common or universal themes in chaos from which we can all learn.

This volume is divided into two parts: "Journey Inward" and "Journey Outward." The first part focuses on the inner life and drama and/or personal issues through which religious leaders are working. The second part focuses on the outward ministry that religious leaders are called to do and all the issues that are disruptive to this calling. The authors are aware of the time of transition that we are all in. In Part II, they seek to address the issues that are causing such disruption for religious leaders as well as the institutions they serve. They will offer suggestions on how to be positive change agents in this world of misinformation, hyper-individualism, tribalism, and social rift. Finally, in the epilogue, the authors write about a historic model of spirituality that has left us signposts of transformation and hope for our own day.

Under the headings of each chapter, the authors have provided queries for self-reflection. As a non-creedal tradition, queries have been used for centuries within the Quaker tradition to help persons and congregations reflect on their personal and corporate spiritual lives. The authors have found them helpful for persons, institutions, and cultures in chaos.

The authors have known each other for more than forty years. Over the course of that time, they have enjoyed many motorcycle trips, shared breakfasts, and opportunities to reflect on each other's life journeys. They have celebrated many joys together as well as supported and counseled one another in times of pain. Along his journey, Mark Minear made the decision to leave the pastoral ministry to pursue his doctorate in counseling psychology. He is a practicing psychologist and has coled *Sacred Chaos* since its inception. Mark is currently on the team of the Des Moines Pastoral Counseling Center in Iowa. James R. (Jim) Newby has been a minister among Friends (Quakers), the United Church of Christ, and the Presbyterian Church (U.S.A.) for more than forty years and is currently serving Cincinnati Friends Meeting in Cincinnati, Ohio, as the minister and public friend.

James R. Newby New Harmony Inn
Mark Minear New Harmony, Indiana

Note

1. Hemingway, Ernest. A *Farewell to Arms*. New York: Charles Scribner's Sons, 1929.

PART I

~

JOURNEY INWARD

1

~

Sharing Pain

Are you willing to share your own pain with others? Do you know when to let your pain plumb the depths of your soul, allowing the pain to help you grow spiritually? Are you sensitive to when it is possible to move beyond your pain to experience newness in life and ministry?

In his classic volume *The Wounded Healer*, Henri J. M. Nouwen writes, "Nobody escapes being wounded. We are all wounded people, whether physically, emotionally, mentally or spiritually. The main question is not, 'How can we hide our wounds?' so we don't have to be embarrassed, but 'How can we put our woundedness in the service of others?' When our wounds cease to be a source of shame, and become a source of healing, we have become wounded healers."[1]

The last sentence is most meaningful in describing an important part of what it means to be a healthy, authentic religious leader: "When our wounds cease to be a source of shame, and become a source of healing . . ." When we stop trying to hide and feel shame for having our pain, when we are able to share our pain with others, we become wounded healers, and when we become wounded healers, becoming authentic with others, a new freedom of openness and ministry is the result.

"When the Wounded Emerge as Healers" was the title of a commencement address that Professor Kimberley C. Patton shared with graduates of Harvard Divinity School. It was published in the *Harvard Divinity Bulletin*. In a very helpful way, her words address the question "What can we learn from the experience of pain?" Speaking directly to the graduates, she said, "Even if a broken heart does not lie in your past or present, it awaits you in your future, at some place, at some time when you will almost certainly be unprepared. But in myth, ritual, and in theology, the broken heart is not a

3

regrettable symptom of derailment, but rather is a starting point of anything that matters. . . . The religious imagination reveals the broken heart as the very best means to wisdom and growth, even when it disrupts the dreams and goals that have inspired us, even when it scatters the ducks we have so carefully lined up in a row."[2]

One who was feeling the effects of having his dreams disrupted and his ducks scattered was Joe.

Now in his early fifties, Joe had been in the ministry for more than twenty-five years—beginning during his seminary years when he was the pastor of a small congregation near his faith tradition's school of theology. He was finding "success" as he moved quite smoothly through four congregations over those years with increasing salaries to match the increasing sizes of the communities of faith, along with the anticipated increasing difficulties; but then he found himself in significant distress in the sixth year of ministry at his fifth church. He was finding considerable resistance to his innovative ideas with a variety of criticisms coming his way. Joe and his wife were struggling in their marriage as well, as the younger of their two children dropped out of college, vocationally lost, in the throes of drug addiction, and angst-filled in the shadow of his older sister. Perhaps most significant, in the midst of all these difficulties, Joe had lost much of his most-trusted sense of creativity in his preaching, his reserve of compassion in his pastoral care, and his strength of confidence-humility in his leadership. Now, after almost two years of being in this dark and lonely place—even feeling estranged from God—all he could imagine were ways to transition out of ministry. Looking back, he was able to see both opportunities in the next congregation that cushioned his need for another honeymoon experience and a pattern of avoidance that had actually served him fairly well. Perhaps he could do only four years of ministry in any one church before he began to hit the wall, feeling the increase of stress and anxiety, and then he would consider another location to serve and flourish briefly once again.

Joe's ducks were indeed scattered. His pain was medicated by avoidance as he was always looking for the greener grass in the next location, the next community of faith. Joe's brokenness was in full view when he came to the *Sacred Chaos* seminar, which is how all of the participants in *Sacred Chaos* come to us. They are unable to see any value to what they are experiencing. They are broken leaders. In the words of one of our participants, "I can no longer lead. . . . All that I can do is follow, going through the motions, meeting my responsibilities, without joy, and without hope for a better future."

A broken heart is not something to be desired; it causes terrible pain. But a broken heart also becomes a softer heart, more aware of the pain of others. Professor Patton writes, "It is highly likely that during such brokenhearted, disorienting times, illusions will shatter, old ideas will be burned up; old ways of being will dissolve and the one thing or person or way of life that we thought we could not live without will be taken from us. These are times when we will learn compassion . . . times when the unbearably wounded will themselves emerge as healers." If the wounds do not turn to bitterness, wounds in the heart can become a place where God works to bring about tenderness and kindness and moves us to compassion. And it is only in retrospect that we are able to identify how a broken heart has moved us to compassion.

I once heard Mary Cosby, cofounder of the Church of the Saviour in Washington, D.C., speak about the need for pain to be shared within a beloved community. She told a story about a new pastor in the church where her mother was an elder. Just prior to his first Sunday, the pastor went to visit Mary's mother and asked her, "If you could say one thing to me before I enter the pulpit of that great church on Sunday morning, what would it be?" She responded, "Remember this: Each person that you see, each pair of eyes that you look into as you are speaking, is sitting beside his or her own pool of tears."

Each of us sits beside our own pool of tears. Some pools are deeper than others, to be sure, but all of us have a pool of our own. Persons who choose to avoid their pain by denial will have difficulty reaching into the hearts of others who are experiencing pain. Pain needs to be brought to speech and shared, and as a result, the tears of transformation will be shed, and we will begin the process of making the chaos we are in become sacred. In the words of the late archbishop Óscar Romero, "There are many things that can only be seen through eyes that have cried."

As difficult as it was for Sarah to share her pain, she was finally able to talk about what she had been experiencing.

All Sarah ever imagined vocationally for herself was becoming a pastor. Growing up in a loving family and feeling close to the Holy Other as long as she could remember, she simply wanted to serve God and God's people. Though her faith tradition had allowed women to be ordained equally alongside men for a few decades, she was quite aware that there were folks in her church, her second assignment since completing seminary, who were still uncomfortable—still getting used to having a woman as a leader; after all, now thirty-four years old, she was the first female clergyperson to ever be a pastor of this 150-year-old congregation. The major moments of discomfort that she experienced from her parishioners were the subtle, sort-of-joking, and not-so-humorous gestures around her singleness. Those parishioners were always trying to set her up with a potential husband. Of course, what was fundamentally painful for Sarah was her need to keep her sexual orientation secret; and though originally she believed that the trade-off was doable and worth it because her denomination did not allow lesbians to be married or ordained, she was finding herself more and more lonely for companionship. This then led to her need to painfully suppress her longings, live increasingly in an inauthentic manner, and face a downward spiral of living a life without her genuine human needs being met. Her incapacity to compensate for her dilemmas any longer had led her to notice an advertisement in the Christian Century *for a* Sacred Chaos *seminar. She arrived with significant questions: 1) Should she abandon the faith tradition of her childhood and explore a tradition more open to the LGBTQ community? 2) Should she remain and stand up for what she believed was a matter of justice—joining others who were also challenging the status quo? 3) Should she depart from service to the local church and transition to chaplaincy or leave organized religion altogether?*

As we have learned from our *Sacred Chaos* participants, the two mistakes that we make with pain are: 1) We spend all our spiritual and emotional energy trying to get out of it, or 2) We perpetuate it because we define our personhood through the eyes of martyrdom. We can avoid a healthy plan of healing and spiritual growth by taking either of these paths. The processing of pain in a healthy way begins when we become sensitive to when it is time to stay on the cross in order to plumb the depths of our spirits, and when it is time to climb down from that cross, prepared to continue along the path of spiritual growth.

Over the years, there have been many models that try to give us a visual understanding of the experience of emotional pain, especially how we have come to recognize the healing journey as one from loss and grief toward acceptance and new beginnings. The model below, "The Quest for Wholeness," is an amalgam of several models along with the author's experience of how facing one's painful and difficult emotions, rather than avoiding or denying them, is the path toward wholeness. It is important to note the difference between wholeness and perfection. Perfection is an ideal that is always out of reach. Wholeness is embracing all that simply is in a person's life—strengths and weaknesses; successes and failures; gifts and vulnerabilities; passions and repulsions; faithfulness and sinfulness. Just as every emotion, painful or pleasant, has something important to tell us or to teach us, every life situation—no matter how enjoyable or how distressful—is part of the overall journey toward the acceptance of the whole of our lives in which everything is welcomed. This is indeed the story of redemption—not about what awaits us on the other side of death, but about what is here and now as part of our ongoing transformation to become the best versions of ourselves as intended by our Creator all along.

THE QUEST FOR WHOLENESS

Healthy

Repentance for hurts
Forgiveness of hurts

Hope

Committing to a
Plan of Discipline

Self-compassion

Sharing our
Stories

Integration

Finding
Community

Wholeness

Awareness

PAIN – Choice ——

Avoidance

Isolation

Estrangement

Turning Inward

Fragmentation

Chronic Distress

Despair

Self-medication

Resentments
and regrets

Unhealthy

As we travel through our seasons of pain in our quest for relief, most of us will jump from the "healthy" to the "unhealthy" and back again many times. It requires a conscious effort to evoke ourselves into sustaining the awareness of pain as avoidance is always the temptation in the moment; and it is the power of this choice that opens the way for the deep and lasting work of healing in our lives. There are periods in our journeys when avoiding or forgetting or denying is the only way that we can survive . . . at least for a while. Hopefully, if we have found our blessed community, we will move back to telling and retelling our stories and continue our journeys toward ongoing transformation and wholeness.

Most of the religious leaders who have come to *Sacred Chaos* have, at first, tried to self-medicate their pain. Over and over, we would hear, "I thought that I could take care of myself. I have helped others through their pain; I truly believed that I could medicate myself to wellness." Self-medication involves many things, from alcohol abuse to extramarital affairs to jumping from one congregation to the next to, in the case of Sarah, living a life of dichotomy in which she felt she needed to keep her sexual identity secret. It seems especially difficult for a religious leader to admit that he or she needs help.

One evening in New Harmony, Indiana, we were in the middle of a *Sacred Chaos* seminar. We were walking after our evening session, sharing with one another how the day's sessions had gone and discussing who needed some special attention the next day. As we walked, we ran into one of our seminar participants, who was on his cell phone. As we approached him, he finished his call and stopped to talk with us. With tears in his eyes and holding his phone in his hand, he said, "I carry two phones." He pulled another one from his pocket to show us. "One I have for calls to my wife and the other one I have for calls to the other woman with whom I am emotionally and sexually involved. I know that my days as a minister are over and that I will soon be leaving my position as the senior minister of the church I am serving. I had no idea my life would become this crazy. I thought I could have it all ways . . . a mistress and a family life. Now I know how stupid I have been. I feel emotionally stuck in a situation from which it is impossible for me to extricate myself. Everything is blowing up in my face."

The pain that this religious leader was having in his personal life was being medicated with an extramarital affair. Throughout our leading of these seminars, we found this to be a common experience. The self-medicating propensity that we human beings have as a coping reaction to pain is well researched. On one level, it is simply a path of avoidance to engage in behaviors that are sufficiently strong, vivid, and intense enough to keep one's attention and to prevent awareness of one's emotional pain and thus choose more healthy ways to respond in order to grow, expand, and be transformed. Though there are a myriad of behaviors that enable a religious leader to suppress such emotional distress, it does appear that certain vulnerabilities are more likely to surface for ministers. Among these reactions are extramarital affairs, substance abuse, and, perhaps for a lack of another descriptor, workaholism.

John seemed to be using all three of the above to help him cope, even though it was destroying his family and ultimately his long-term capacity to serve the church. He found himself angling for attention from women in his congregation, and, as a result, he allowed himself to be in situations in which lines were crossed. Evenings with his alcohol became more and more a steady habit, along with some notion that this is what he needed to do to be able to sleep at night. Unfortunately, the alcohol helped him sleep for only three to four hours before being disrupted. Between the sleep deprivation over time and pouring himself into busyness at the church (which also had its rewards of accolades from parishioners), John was in an unsustainable cycle. Of course, the chronic sleep deprivation did not allow John to be very efficient with his time and energy. What it did do was open the way for workaholism, coupled with compulsive behaviors that gave him the illusion that he was working hard on behalf of his congregation. He arrived at Sacred Chaos acknowledging that he was in an unsustainable pattern.

I believe that it was the late John Chancellor of NBC News who said, "If you want to make God laugh, tell God your plans." He made this statement at the time of his retirement, when he had just learned that he had terminal cancer. Life is filled with such pain and tragedy, when plans that we have made get thwarted because of an unexpected turn of events. Persons with whom we have planned and with whom we have worked side by side die too soon. Relationships that once seemed solid fall apart. Promises that we felt were sure and impregnable are not kept. Hope can quickly become hopelessness.

The future is never sure, and the present is always in a state of flux. The only thing about which we can be sure is that things are *not sure*. One of the reasons I founded the *Sacred Chaos* seminar was because of the chaos I experienced in my own life. At a particular time in my journey, life seemed like a straight path, today passing into tomorrow, sure, secure, and predictable. The straight path I was on was one of problem-fixer and caretaker. The more I was needed to fix things, the more my life felt justified. Nothing seemed to be beyond my capability. The course of my life could be compared to the person who performs in the circus by spinning plates on sticks. Just as I finished adding a new plate, the first stick needed another twist to keep its plate spinning. Whether it was my marriage, fatherhood, or my ministry, there seemed to be no end to the number of plates I could add to my life.

My wife would meet me at the door of our home with an airline ticket and a clean bag of clothes, while she took a bag of dirty clothes and a used airline ticket from my hands. The way I could keep everything spinning seemed amazing. My workaholism medicated my pain, and I received added strength when someone would affirm me by saying, "Jim, I don't know how you do it all!" I didn't either.

And then my father died, and my mother was diagnosed with severe dementia. Our only daughter left for college in Michigan, and my mentor died, a man with whom I had worked closely for fifteen years. My life was becoming chaotic. As I was struggling ever more diligently to keep the plates spinning, I went through a divorce, which completed my litany of loss and sent me to the floor with plates crashing down all around.

My story is not uncommon from the stories we have heard in *Sacred Chaos*. All religious leaders experience loss. All know or will know pain. Religious leaders know how much the institutions they serve love workaholism, and how the more that they do the more they are rewarded by the institution. Unfortunately, if there is not the adequate self-care needed to balance the work and ministry extended to others, chaos in one's life will erupt.

Reflecting on the new realities that chaos forces upon us, there are ways to begin the healing process. As the illustration "The Quest for Wholeness" shows, avoidance, isolation, and denying our pain can be our first response. The more quickly we recognize and name our pain, however, the more quickly we will begin the process of healing. That said, God has given us an amazing array of ways to cope with what life deals us, and in some circumstances when our pain is overwhelming, avoidance or turning inward may be the only way we can survive. If it becomes a permanent state, however, the suppression of pain will overwhelm us, and it will eventually destroy our ability to function. And so, overall, the deeper and faster we face and move into our pain, the sooner we can begin the healing process. As Thomas Merton has written, "The truth that many people never understand until it is too late is that the more you try to avoid suffering the more you suffer."[3] And Richard Rohr reminds us, "If we do not transform our pain, we will most assuredly transmit it—usually to those closest to us: Our family, our neighbors, our co-workers, and, invariably, the most vulnerable, our children."[4]

Becoming aware of our pain is the first step in the healing process. Another step is being able to *forgive* those persons and institutions that we feel have harmed us. As we accept our pain, being open and honest about what we are feeling and experiencing, we will learn that forgiveness can be a primary factor in making the pain bearable. Forgiveness is not just a medication for our pain but also a *process* that can lead to healing our souls.

A beautiful illustration of forgiveness comes from my friend African American singer Tom Tipton, whose biography I wrote a few years ago. Tom grew up in Washington, D.C., where his first job was to shine shoes in front of the White House. One day he heard someone talking about the annual Easter Egg Roll on the White House lawn, and how children were all invited to participate. This was during the administration of Franklin D. Roosevelt. Tom told his mother about this event, and so she dressed him in his best clothes and escorted him to the White House. At the gate, Tom and his mother were told that they were not allowed to join the other children because he was Black. His mother silently walked Tom back home, and when arriving home Tom told his father about what he had experienced. The elder Mr. Tipton placed Tom on his knee and said, "Don't worry about this and do not let it get you down. Forgive the man at the White House gate. There will be other parties you can attend. You just work on being the best person that you know how to be and the best shoeshine boy that you can be, and be grateful to God for the gifts that you have."[5] Tom did forgive this overt example of discrimination. Later in life, he would give two commanding performances inside the White House for two different presidents. Early in life, Tom learned about the spiritual importance of forgiveness, and by practicing it, he was able to stay out of a prison of bitterness.

Forgiveness is central to both Judaism and Christianity. Most notable within the Jewish tradition is the Year of Jubilee, when debts are forgiven and former debtors are given an opportunity to begin anew. Within the Christian tradition is the response of Jesus to Peter's question "How many times, Lord, must I forgive? Till seven times?" Jesus responds, "Not seven times, but seventy times seven" (Matthew 18:21–22). In other words, forgiveness is to become a part of who we are. No one can forgive that many times without forgiveness becoming a basic tenet in his or her life.

I love the story about the little girl who came downstairs from her bedroom and found her mother making breakfast. The little girl said to her mother, "I dreamed about Jesus last night."

"Oh, you did, did you."

"Yes," said the little girl. "He told me that you had confessed to him all of your sins."

"Really," said the mother, now more intrigued with the little girl's dream. "And what sins did Jesus tell you that I confessed?"

The little girl responded, "He said that he had forgotten."

Coupled with forgiveness is an attitude of repentance. There are at least two things in life that cannot be overdone—*expressions of gratitude* and *expressions of repentance*. And yet how hard it is to repent. Aleksandr Solzhenitsyn, who was imprisoned in a Russian gulag for exercising free speech, wrote, "The gift of repentance distinguishes human beings from the animal world. The habit of repentance is lost to our whole callous and chaotic age."[6]

All of us have harmed others over the years. "I am sorry" cannot be said too often. It frees the soul from the darkness of blame and the defensiveness of the hurt we feel. It is all right to express justified anger, but when such anger is wrapped in vengeance and a defensive transference of responsibility for our lot in life, then it will harm our souls. As Melody Beattie has written, "Real power comes when we stop holding others responsible for our pain, and we take responsibility for all our feelings."[7]

Forgiveness and repentance are both important parts of the healing process. For persons in pain, a natural response is to lash out at others, wounding their hearts. So many unnecessary wounds have been inflicted by those who have not made forgiveness and repentance part of their healing process. I have been helped by the wisdom from *Zorba the Greek*, who tells of an old neighbor he knew as a child: "One day he took me on his knee and placed his hand on my hand as though he were giving me his blessing. 'Alexis,' he said, 'I'm going to tell you a secret. You are too small to understand now, but you'll understand when you are bigger. Listen, little one: Neither the seven stories of heaven nor the seven stories of earth are enough to contain God; but a person's heart can contain God. So be very careful, Alexis, and may my blessing go with you—never to wound a person's heart.'"[8]

Recently I received an email from someone who told me that I had hurt his feelings. I thought long and hard about my recent interactions with this person, retracing our conversations. For the life of me, I could not figure out how I had hurt him. And yet he *felt* that I had caused him pain. My response, without apologizing for what I had said or had done, was *to apologize for the wounding of his heart*. I told him, "It was never my intention to wound your heart. I am so sorry for what I did or said that has caused you such pain. Please forgive me." Asking for forgiveness does not mean that you deny what you said, especially if you feel strongly about the issue at hand. Also, forgiving others does not mean that those who have harmed you can get away with the pain that they have caused. In both instances, what it *does* mean is that you can begin to move into the future in a *new* way that is, hopefully, free from animosity. It was Nelson Mandela who said as he left prison, "As I walked out the door toward the gate that would lead to my freedom, I knew if I didn't leave my bitterness and hatred behind, I'd still be in prison." This is true for emotional prisons as well as physical prisons.

Forgiveness and *repentance* are two important aspects of the healing process. And so is *patience*. It is impossible to force the pain that we are going through into healing. To evoke the soul out of the painful past and into the present and future possibility of healing is not something that is done hurriedly or all at once. Soul-aches are different from headaches, for which you can take a pill and the pain goes away. Soul-aches require patience. As one of my spiritual counselors said to me, "Let the pain you are feeling plumb the depths of your soul." She was encouraging me to learn the lessons my pain was teaching me . . . lessons that have been learned by others who have experienced pain through the centuries. If we are fortunate, we will become more compassionate to our fellow humans along this journey of life. We will find ourselves doing the things we used to make fun of and walking away from those things we used to do. Meaningful relationships in community, seeking peace both within ourselves and between individuals and nations, and working for justice and equality for all will become obsessions. An increasing sensitivity toward the entire created order will tug at our hearts, and we will come to understand that we are one part of this creation, rather than believing that we have control and dominion over the creation.

Healing our pain is a continuous process of learning how to allow love into our hurting hearts. We will never be free of pain for it is a basic ingredient of life. Each pain experienced carries a special place in our hearts not to be forgotten. When we process our pain, bringing it to speech, sharing it with others by telling and retelling our stories, forgiving and repenting and recognizing that healing takes patience, we can begin to make the pain bearable. Pain will come but it will never entirely go. We need not be frantic as the ambiguities and pain of life are thrust upon us. God loves and suffers with us, and in the midst of the calamity occurring in our lives, we are surrounded by the love of God.

Notes

1. Nouwen, Henri J. M. *The Wounded Healer: Ministry in Contemporary Society.* New York: Doubleday Image Books, 1972.

2. Patton, Kimberley C. "When the Wounded Emerge as Healers." Cambridge: *Harvard Divinity Bulletin*, Winter 2006.

3. Merton, Thomas. *Love and Living.* Edited by Naomi Burton Stone and Brother Patrick Hart. New York: Bantam Books, 1979.

4. Rohr, Richard. Daily meditation, October 17, 2018.

5. Newby, James R. *Shining Out and Shining In: Understanding the Life Journey of Tom Tipton.* Bloomington: AuthorHouse, 2013.

6. Deavel, David P. and Wilson, Jessica Hooten. *Solzhenitsyn and American Culture: The Russian Soul in the West.* South Bend: University of Notre Dame Press, 2020.

7. Beattie, Melody. *The Language of Letting Go: Daily Meditations on Codependency.* San Francisco: HarperCollins, 1990.

8. Kazantzakis, Nikos. *Zorba the Greek.* New York: Simon and Schuster, 1953.

2

⁓

Recovering Passion

How have you sought to recover your passion in your ministry? How do you experience passion? What do you feel when you lose passion?
The first casualty of the experience of pain is passion. Because of the pain they are experiencing, most of our *Sacred Chaos* participants have lost their passion for ministry, and with the loss of passion there is a corresponding loss of a sense of meaning. What is life without a sense of meaning and a passion that gives it vitality?

At our best, human beings want more than mere existence and *need* more than mere existence. In our seminars, we share with participants the idea of the 80/20 rule of life. We know that some life experiences will drain and de-energize us. About 20 percent of life can be called "grunt" work, and grunt work can be de-energizing. If we can have passion for 80 percent of our life experiences, we remain spiritually and emotionally healthy. When the ratio becomes 70/30 or 60/40, then we can get into trouble with our emotions and spirit. There have been times when I have felt my passion for life waning and dipping into a place that is not healthy, and there have been times when I was so filled with passion for what I was doing that it could barely be contained. I would suppose that this is true for most people.

For those who know me, it is no secret that I dislike long meetings that focus mainly on institutional governance. At this particular time in my life, I am the Clerk of the Committee on Training and Recording of the Wilmington Yearly Meeting of the Religious Society of Friends. (We care for and train new ministers who feel called to the ministry.) We are in the process of rewriting and editing the manual about sexual harassment. It is work that has to be done, I know, but the long hours of sitting with my colleagues, going over each line with a fine-tooth comb, is a de-energizing experience. It robs me of my ministerial passion. For me, this is part of my 20 percent.

And then there are those other things in ministry that give ministers passion. The other evening, I was talking with a Presbyterian minister who had just completed her third memorial service in one week. I would have expected her to tell me that she was drained, and that the stress of such ministry was taking its toll on her emotional and spiritual health. Instead, she shared with me that it is the ministry of grief, sitting with the families who have lost a loved one and walking with them through the memories of the departed, that gives her life passion. She is now in a process of discerning where her next call will take her. I would assume that she will be seeking out a position as a minister of pastoral care.

"Passion" can be an elusive word, much like the word "spirituality." That said, I can try to work out some rather broad definitive parameters. Our English term "passion" comes from the Latin *"passio,"* which can be defined as "overwhelming emotion." Such emotion will be experienced in many ways throughout life, whether in sorrow and suffering or happiness and joy. In all ways, passion will carry within it the element of intensity, whether this intensity is an experience of great sorrow or great joy. Some will experience passion as the fuel that ignites a search for a more meaningful existence, or as the stimulus to drive toward an ideal. Most of us will recognize when we are experiencing passion in our lives, and we will most certainly recognize its absence.

Donald was a *Sacred Chaos* participant who had lost his passion. He had just gone through a divorce, and the church he was serving was not supportive. It seemed to Donald that he could do nothing right. When we met him, he told us that he was just about ready to turn in his clerical collar for some brown shorts and become a delivery driver.

Though many factors had converged to bring Donald to a point of resignation, not just from his local congregation but also from his vocation as a religious leader, the tipping point was his divorce. He recognized that it likely was his preoccupation with succeeding as a minister that led to the thinning of his intimacy with his wife. The divorce itself, however, felt like a catastrophic failure, one from which he could not recover. How could he lead his congregation into nurturing, healthy relationships when he was unable to maintain the intimate connection in his own marriage? His passion to serve was crushed, and he was immobilized. Whether it was his own damaged self-perception or some of the negative feedback sent his way, those reasons seemed to him sufficient for him to resign. As a last resort, Donald came to a Sacred Chaos seminar to see what might be possible for him—how he could comfortably leave his sense of being called by God to ministry for a non-ministerial job that would provide him with a major reduction of stress. He wanted something in which he did not have to emotionally bring his work home with him. He was desperate for work that would help him regain his passion for life.

There are many things that can cause the loss of passion in life and ministry. Here are some examples that we have gleaned from the ministers under our care:

The loss of passion is the result of *living a life of dichotomy* or living out someone else's story. When we live out someone else's expectations of how we should be living, or when we mask ourselves and hide the reality of who we truly are, we pay with a loss of passion.

During a seminar I led on *spiritual autobiography*, one of the participants remarked, "I've just realized that I have been living out my father's story rather than my own!" One step in passion recovery begins with the recognition that there are many of us who are living lives of dichotomy, trying to be the selves others want us to be rather than being our *real* selves.

Sam Keen is a mythologist who leads seminars on storytelling. During one of his seminars, I heard him use this illustration: Using the language of the computer age, he talked about how each of us is equipped with "hard drives." As we mature, we are constantly being given "software," the stories of family, the stories of culture, the stories of our religion, until we find ourselves living out all the stories that others have given us. Keen's point was that our mental and spiritual health requires us to discover our *own* stories and learn what is separating us from those stories. This does not mean rejecting all the stories that we have been given in this life. That would be an impossible task to undertake even if we tried. It does mean, however, that in order to be spiritually and emotionally healthy, we need to become conscious of what has been given to us rather than unconsciously live out others' stories and expectations.

Another way our lives are de-energized and we lose passion is closely associated with *the fears that govern our lives.* It was during a visit at the University of Oxford with the late Anglican bishop Stephen Neill that I first learned that "fear not" and "do not be afraid" are the most common expressions in the Bible. The longer I live, the more I am convinced that fear is the greatest hindrance to spiritual growth and a life lived in passion. Fear keeps us trapped in deadening life patterns that we repeat over and over again—the fear of rejection, the fear of economic failure, the fear of vulnerability, the fear of change and the disruption of the well-patterned lives that we have made for ourselves, the fear of loss of job, loss of marriage, loss of family, loss of all those things that keep us feeling secure, content, and comfortable. And then there is the fear of being seen and understood for who we truly are rather than the false selves we have anxiously projected. Finally, there is the *big fear*, the fear of death and dying. All our fears keep us from experiencing life in all of its abundance, leaving us trapped within a cell of our own making and going through the motions of living but not living fully.

In her book *Journey to the Heart*, Melody Beattie writes, "Fear can be like a brick wall on our path. We may want to move forward . . . we want to feel better, do something new, live differently, go to the next place on our journey . . . but if we have unrecognized fears about that, we may feel like we've hit a wall. We don't know we're afraid; the fear is tucked and hidden away. All we can see is that, for some unknown reason, we can't seem to move forward in life . . . or we may be conscious of our fear, but be refusing to deal with it." She continues, "Gently face your fears, one at a time as they arise, then release its energy; let it dissipate into thin air. Don't be afraid of what you'll find; the feeling is only fear."[1]

Another way in which we lose our passion is by living in the history of the *"what if"s and "if only"s of life*. I love the definition of the forgiveness of oneself: "True forgiveness of oneself is finally giving up all hope of having a different past." How many of us waste days and even years unable to forgive ourselves, paying homage to the god of regret?

In his book *How Good Do We Have to Be?* Rabbi Harold S. Kushner tells how Carl Rogers, the famous psychologist, would approach a therapeutic encounter: "There is something I do before I start a session. I let myself know that I am enough. Not perfect. Perfect would not be enough. But that I am human, and that is enough. There is nothing this patient can do or feel that I can't feel myself, I can be with him, I am enough."[2] Knowing that we are not perfect is important to healing and the recovery of passion. *We are enough.*

The loss of passion also is associated with the *baggage of guilt* that so many of us carry in our backpacks of life. How many lives have been short-circuited because of the feelings of guilt that are embedded within each of us? And it is one thing to recognize guilt, and another thing to do something about it.

We all know people, friends, parents, spouses, and ministers and priests, who are gifted at inducing a spiritually destructive and passion-killing guilt into our lives. Such guilt keeps us from living life fully and filled with passion. May we not only learn to recognize our feelings of guilt but also find a way to move beyond them and into the light of good mental and spiritual health.

Passion in one's ministry also can be jeopardized by all *the little things that can occupy our time*, as well as, and I apologize if this is too harsh, the *irritating congregants* who will not leave us alone. (A friend refers to this type of congregant as an EGR—Extra Grace Required!) I recently had lunch on a

Monday with a colleague who was lamenting what he had to deal with on the Sunday before. His practice is to get to his church about an hour before the beginning of the education hour, which precedes worship. As he was making the final preparations on his sermon for that morning, he received a text from a high school friend. A few weeks ago, he had the hard task of telling this friend that he is not allowed to sleep in his car overnight in the church parking lot. The trustees of his church did not allow it, and if his car was seen in the lot overnight, concerned neighbors would likely call the police. His friend did not take this well, and ever since he had been berating my colleague via text. Texting has made the world a more communicative community, and it also has made the lives of ministers more difficult. Feelings of animosity can be delivered instantaneously, any time of the day or night. And so many of us respond to that little "ding" sound our phones make when we receive new messages, like Pavlov's dogs. And so this high school friend of my ministerial colleague had become a constant nemesis via text.

And then, following this first text, he received another text from a congregant who is upset about the mask policy at his church. This, of course, is a new irritant since COVID-19 . . . the divisions within a congregation over masks and vaccines. There is a public health committee within this minister's church, and so he does not set this policy alone. He is, however, the most visible presence in support of continuing the wearing of masks even if one is vaccinated. The person texting my minister friend said he was "living in fear."

On the Saturday night before, my minister colleague received word that the hospitality committee of his congregation had decided that they would no longer try to serve coffee and cookies after worship because the mask policy was infringing on their ability to be hospitable.

Finally, my colleague said that after worship on his drive home, one of the nursery workers had left some food in a plastic bag on a table in the nursery and asked if he wouldn't mind putting it in the refrigerator for her. Listening to my friend's litany of the little things in his stressful life made me think of Simon Sinek's statement "Working hard for something we don't care about is called *stress*. Working hard for something we love is called *passion*."[3] Juggling all these things on a Sunday, as well as preparing to lead worship and provide a message of hope to the many hopeless souls in the pews, can lead to a loss of passion. Here is an anecdotal observation: *When the world's problems are overwhelming, we tend to focus way too much on the little things because we feel we can at least control these.*

"They didn't teach me about these things in seminary" is a familiar refrain we hear in our *Sacred Chaos* seminars. One of the most bizarre experiences of ministry was shared with us by Devon. He was feeling a loss of passion in his role as minister and was doing the best he could to function as he sought to avoid a full-on case of depression. One day he was called by the neighbor of one of his parishioners and was told that Emma, a member of his church, had just experienced a house fire. He immediately went to the scene, where the fire department was still putting out some of the smoldering embers. The house was a complete loss. He found his parishioner, a woman who was in her nineties, wandering around in the backyard in her robe and slippers. He sought to console her as she looked upon the horrific scene of what was once her home. She kept saying, "I can't find Malcolm. I can't find Malcolm." While consoling her, Devon was able to learn that Malcolm was her cat. So, Devon told her that he would go look for the cat. After about an hour of walking around the rubble of the burned house, he found Malcolm, who, unfortunately, had burned to death in the fire. Again, Devon sought to console his congregant, and after a while, he volunteered to bury Malcolm in the backyard. And so here was Devon, feeling depressed himself, consoling his ninety-something-year-old congregant and making a hole in the backyard to bury Malcolm. Sometimes ministry involves the burying of a cat.

Maintaining one's passion as a religious leader can be difficult. Recovering passion once it is lost can be *very* difficult. There are ways, however, to begin the process of passion recovery, which also will help as we continue to process the pain that cost us our passion. We have made a start on finding the passion we are missing when we connect with others in the formation of community. Finding connection in this disconnected world has never been more difficult, but I believe that community, a *beloved* community, can be formed to move us to new places spiritually.

We know that we can be creative alone, but when we can share our stories, our faith, our dreams and vision with like-minded pilgrims, the creativity is enhanced and the passion for such creativity is revived. We can worship God alone, but when we worship within a beloved community of like-hearted seekers, the worship experience goes deeper.

The creation of a beloved community, in which meaning in life can be sought and passion for life and ministry can be recovered, can take many and varied forms. There are, however, certain elements that are helpful in the formation process.

First, community is formed when we gather together, two, three, or five hundred, and experience the transforming, life-changing power of a Spirit beyond our finitude. We have found that worship based on silence is the most effective kind of worship for our *Sacred Chaos* participants. One of the most difficult disciplines for persons in chaos is to sit still. Seeking to quiet the racing mind and spirit and allow the Spirit to wash over one's troubled heart and settle one's anxiety is one of the goals of worship.

Silence has always played the central role in my own spiritual development, and whenever I have been in chaos, I have returned to silence as a helpful means to move me to new places spiritually. As the son of a Quaker minister, I began each First Day (Sunday to the world beyond Quakers) by "going to meeting." As we would find our regular seats in the little Friends meetinghouse in Minneapolis, Minnesota, my mother would turn to me and my siblings, raise her finger to her lips, and politely shush us. This was followed by the familiar words that every Quaker knows by heart, "It is time to center down and mind the Light." I knew the routine, and early in life I learned that in this experience of quiet-seeking, the sacred and the human could meet. It was hallowed ground.

For our *Sacred Chaos* participants, we begin each morning by saying, "It is time to center down and mind the Light." For thirty minutes, we sit in silence and worship. Through the experience of worshipping together, community is formed.

Another element of passion-recovering community has to do with the tradition of storytelling. When we tell and retell our stories of the meaningful experiences of our lives and gather together our memories to share with others, community forms. The stories we share with one another keep the fire of fellowship ablaze. In the Gospel of Luke, chapter 24, the disciples remember and tell the story of how their master walked with them on the Emmaus road, and in verse 32 they exclaim, "Did not our hearts burn within us while he talked to us on the road, while he opened to us the Scriptures?" *Remembering* helped the disciples form community via shared experience. We recover passion when we tell and retell the stories of our lives and our traditions.

A beloved community also is a place where we can share our pain, and it is also a place where we can help process the pain of others. We create community when the pain that we carry can be shared. In the words of the Apostle Paul, "If one member suffers, all suffer together" (1 Corinthians 12:26).

Community also is created when we encourage one another and build one another up. We live in an overly critical time. Religious leaders are especially prone to criticism as they try to serve a wide diversity of persons who are living on the edges of their emotional and spiritual issues. And I have never met a religious leader who is not a people pleaser. We went into the ministry because we care. Our lives are defined by the caregiving that we do. The truth is, however, that we cannot please *everyone*. People bring their critical spirits into the religious arena, and the religious leaders become the main focus. "The sermon was dull and did not meet my spiritual needs."

"I was sick and the minister did not call on me." "The minister speaks too much about racial justice and the poor." "I don't like the way the minister dresses." And one I heard recently about a female colleague: "Her earrings are too large, and they dangle too low!" Finding fault comes easily, and passion for one's ministry can quickly wane when one is under assault. Within the beloved community, however, negative criticism has no place. Again, the Apostle Paul speaks to our condition: "Encourage one another and build one another up" (1 Thessalonians 5:11).

Being in community is hard work because relationships are hard work. Passion recovery is dependent upon our being able to share our issues within a beloved community. When we come together through a transformative experience with the Infinite, telling and retelling our stories, processing one another's pain by listening empathetically to one another, and practicing the ministry of encouragement, we will be about the task of passion recovery.

Another avenue that is helpful as we seek to recover our passion is spiritual friendship. Although the creation of a beloved community and living as a part of such a community are helpful, they do not negate the importance of discovering at least one person who can be a true spiritual friend. Taking the risk of openly sharing a spiritual kinship with another person places one in a vulnerable position. And yet this vulnerability is worth the risk if it keeps the passion for life and ministry ever vibrant. Our souls yearn for more than physical presence or humorous anecdotes. We need more than a lunch partner or a colleague who will never share more than amusing political or social commentary. Passion recovery requires a friendship that is without pretense and without the fear of expressing deep emotion. This is a friendship that is centered in the spiritual union of souls, wherein nothing is considered too personal, too sacred, too outrageous, or too emotionally disturbing to be shared together.

Henri Nouwen and Fred Rogers were spiritual friends who wrote back and forth to one another for years. In a post on Facebook, Adam Baker notes that at one point, Mr. Rogers sent Nouwen a particularly discouraging article that had been written about Mr. Rogers. As Baker notes, "Words like these, attacking Fred's character and questioning his intentions, were deeply wounding to him." Of course, Nouwen knew about human pain and was a very comforting personality. Nouwen replied to Mr. Rogers, saying,

> It must be really painful to be confronted with a total misunderstanding of your mission and your spiritual intentions. It is these little persecutions within the church that hurt the most. . . . They come and will keep coming precisely when you do something significant for the Kingdom. It has always struck me that the

real pain comes often from the people from whom we expected real support. It was Jesus' experience and the experience of all the great visionaries in the Church, and it continues to be the experience of many who are committed to Jesus. . . . Some of the criticisms we simply have to suffer and see as invitations to enter deeper into the heart of Jesus. . . . Let us pray for one another, that we would remain faithful and kind, not becoming bitter or angry in such a way that our hearts would harden within us. Instead, may we encourage one another to return to the center—to Jesus . . . helping joy and peace find root in our lives in ways that this world may not understand.[4]

Religious leaders need the kind of spiritual friendship that Fred Rogers and Henri Nouwen shared together.

When I lived in Des Moines, Iowa, and was the minister for spiritual growth at Plymouth Congregational Church, I belonged to a group of five men who would meet for breakfast every other Saturday morning. It was in that group that I learned about spiritual friendship and how important it is to my spiritual growth to be able to be open and vulnerable about what is going on in my life. Confidentiality and trust were the keys to the group's success as each of us grew together in love and support of one another. When I left Des Moines for the Twin Cities, an important part of my life went missing. It has been only since the pandemic that I have been able to rejoin the group and pick up where we left off. For all the negatives associated with this pandemic, Zoom is one of those things for which I am grateful. Last week, one of our group was able to join us from Mumbai, India, and others joined from Des Moines and Cincinnati, Ohio. The point is that such spiritual friendships do not have to end when one physically moves away. Zoom technology has made it possible to stay connected from anywhere in the world.

Trusting one another in a spiritual friendship takes courage. We are vulnerable when we trust. We could get hurt. And yet there are worse things than getting hurt, such as to close oneself off from the possibility of a passion-reviving spiritual friendship because we fear trusting. Our quest for passion in life and ministry means that we will have to take risks.

Recovering passion in one's life and ministry is a multifaceted process. Connecting with a community of like-minded and like-hearted persons, as well as connecting with one, two, or five spiritual friends whom we can trust with our story, are two parts of the path toward such passion recovery. Another important part is to go beyond our normal cultural context, interacting with people outside our usual circle of operation. For the most part, religious leaders tend to stay within the boundaries of their faith communities. Breaking out of these boundaries and seeing the life and activity that lie beyond can be a liberating and passion-recovering experience.

While I was going through some of my most difficult times in chaos, I would venture out of my culture and interact with persons in my neighborhood pub. Here I found a culture completely different from the safety of the faith community. Many were hardworking laborers who would stop on their way home for beer and conversation with friends. It was a real-life *Cheers*, where everybody knew your name. Here I met many persons who were experiencing all levels of brokenness, and I could interact with them in their "safe" place. Beyond sharing the stories of sports and business ventures, which often served as veneers for their pain, the people who came to this pub were hurting, seeking connection, and looking for others who would hear their stories. Here they would not be condemned for their human failures. I loved being a part of such a community beyond the church. To this day, I maintain friendships with those I met in a place religious leaders tend to avoid.

I am reminded of the words of Lord George MacLeod, the founder of the IONA Fellowship:

> I simply argue that the cross should be raised at the center of the marketplace as well as on the steeple of the church. I am recovering the claim that Jesus was not crucified in a cathedral between two candles, but on a cross between two thieves; on the town's garbage heap; at a crossroad so cosmopolitan they had to write his title in Hebrew and Latin and Greek . . . at the kind of place where cynics talk smut, and thieves curse, and soldiers gamble. Because that is where he died. And that is what he died for. And that is what he died about. That is where Christians ought to be and what Christians ought to be about.

What my pub life did for me was help me put my life in perspective. When we are in chaos, it is easy to assume that we are the only ones with problems and the only ones experiencing such pain. Of course, we are not. What I learned was how the pain I was going through is a universal experience. The way one goes through it is unique because you are the one feeling it. But we all have pain. My experience in the pub reinforced this truth and helped me gain a new perspective on my issues. I remember one time when I was sitting with my therapist and I was reciting my litany of loss. He sat patiently listening, as any good therapist would do. Finally, when there was a lull in my monologue, he looked me in the eye and said, "Welcome to the human race."

Beyond such culture changes at home as a visit to the local pub, one can be about the task of passion recovery by leaving North America for a visit to another country, a country that does not have all the material advantages of the United States. Again, this kind of experience will put your life and pain in perspective. I remember the culture shock when I first traveled to Mexico. I can still feel and taste the poverty in the little villages and the chaos of Mexico City. One evening, I left my hotel in Mexico City and walked to a nearby restaurant. All along the three short blocks to the restaurant, I was accosted by children and mothers begging for money from what they considered to be a rich North American. Comparatively speaking, I *was* a rich North American. There was one little girl who I have never been able to get out of my mind. She was crippled with a broken leg that had never been repaired. Hobbling beside her mother, she would reach her hand out for anything that I could give her. I asked my guide and companion who was traveling with me, and who was a native of Mexico, why the little girl had never had her leg set and repaired. His answer was numbing: "Because her mother knows that a crippled child can get more money from North Americans than a child who has no physical problems." Perspective. . . . The contrast between the culture in which I was reared and in which I was living and the poverty-stricken lives of those I encountered in Mexico was life changing and passion recovering. Deep down in the recesses of my heart, I felt God moving within me, transforming me to find myself outside of myself and my culture. As a result, a whole new life was in the offing.

Reynolds Price wrote a book about his new life and the life-changing vision he experienced. He had a tumor that had developed in his spinal cord, wrapping itself around the nerves in his upper back. About a month after his surgery to remove the tumor, Price had what he calls "a happening." One moment he was resting in his bed, and the next moment he was in first-century Palestine on the shore of the Sea of Galilee. In this vision, Price sees Jesus moving his way, gently inviting him to follow Jesus out into the sea. Here, in detail, is how he describes the transforming vision that he experienced: "We waded out into the cool lake water twenty feet from shore until we stood waist-deep. Jesus silently took up handfuls of water and poured them over my head and back till water ran down my surgical scar. Then he spoke, saying, 'Your sins are forgiven,' and turned to shore again, done with me. I came on behind him, thinking in standard greedy fashion, 'It's not my sins I'm worried about.' And so I asked, 'Am I also cured?' Jesus turned to face me, and finally said two words, 'that too.'"[5] Price titled his book *A Whole New Life*. In an interview about his book for the *Oxford Review*, he said,

"When you undergo huge traumas in middle life, everybody is in league with us to deny that the old life is ended. . . . Everybody is trying to patch us up and get us back to who we were, when in fact what we need to be told is, *'You're dead. Who are you going to be tomorrow?'"*[6] (italics added).

Processing our pain and recovering the passion that we have lost because of our pain will lead to transformation. All those persons and institutions that have come to know us in a certain and predictable way will be thrown out of their orbits. "Everybody is trying to patch us up and get us back to who we were," says Price. This has been my experience as well. The truth is, the old has gone; behold the new! *Transformation.* . . . As we tell our *Sacred Chaos* participants, what transformation may mean for you is that you may walk away from your work as a religious leader. This is one of the risks of recovering passion. What we always emphasize, however, is this: *Walking away from professional ministry does not mean walking away from God or meaning in life.* In fact, your true meaning in life may lie beyond professional ministry and the institution you have been serving.

To get at the heart of understanding God and how God wants us to live, asking questions is central. At its root, to question is to be on a *quest.* Whether we recognize it or not, we are all on a journey to discern who God is, why we are here, and how we can live so that we not only have life but also have a life that is meaningful and filled with passion.

As we face the myriad of choices moving through our journey of chaos, passion recovery, and transformation, we can be helped by keeping certain queries in mind and heart. Queries lead to self-reflection, and self-reflection can take us on the path to new life. Throughout my experience in ministry, many people have come to me seeking guidance about what their professional vocations should be. They want to be sure that they will be doing what God wants them to do. This is why it can be very difficult for a religious leader to leave his or her chosen vocation, because the leader does not know how to walk away from a "call" that he or she thought God had instigated. My counsel has always been that I don't think God really cares about the particulars in your life choices, but there are certain things about which I believe God does care, and those things are important as we make the choices we do. Those in our *Sacred Chaos* seminars have found the following queries helpful in their discernment process:

1. Are *love* and *care* part of the vocational choice I am making?
   A life of meaning that is filled with passion is found in the many great and small acts of love and care we do for one another. Religious leaders become religious leaders because love and care are central to who they

are. Love and care, however, should not be relegated to just one profession. These are things that we can do regardless of chosen vocation.

2. Is the choice I am making one in which *truth* and *integrity* are present?

Truth and integrity should be at the core of who we are as persons and who we believe God is as Spirit. One of the first casualties when one finds himself or herself in chaos is integrity. If we make a choice in which our integrity is compromised and from which truth is absent, we can assume that such a choice is not part of a God-centered meaningful life.

3. Is the choice I am making one that promotes the cause of *justice* and *righteousness* in the world?

God's first requirement as expressed in Micah 6:8 is "to do justice." If we believe that God is a God of justice, then we are called to expose injustice and work for justice whenever and wherever we can. The Prophet Amos declared, "Let justice roll down like waters, and righteousness like an ever-flowing stream" (Amos 5:24). A meaningful and passion-filled life involves choices that lead to acts of justice and righteousness for all people.

4. Is the choice I am making one in which *beauty* and a sense of *awe* find expression?

As I remember the story, when he first set his eyes on the Alps, Baron Friedrich von Hügel exclaimed, "I didn't want to *climb* them. I didn't want to *own* them. I didn't want to *mine* them. All that I wanted to do was to *adore* them." And describing the redwoods in California, John Steinbeck wrote in *Travels with Charley*, "From them come silence and awe."[7] God is present in all that lifts our spirits into a sense of awe. Life experiences that put our souls in a place where we know true spiritual beauty, whether that beauty is found in persons or in nature, connect us with the Living God. In the sense of awe that results, the process of passion recovery is enhanced, and we move forward toward a more meaningful life.

In the end, only time will bring us to the new life filled with passion that we seek. As with the processing of pain, be *patient* with yourself. Remain focused on the spiritual, recognizing that the transition you are in is a gift from God. Be respectful of the old patterns that have served you well in your former life while at the same time recognizing that the recovery of passion will require new ways. "Don't ask yourself what the world needs," said Howard Thurman. "Ask yourself what makes you come alive and then go do that. Because what the world needs is people who have come alive."[8] In time, not in your time but in God's time, a new passion will emerge. We believe in a God of new beginnings, and of these new beginnings there is no end.

Notes

1. Beattie, Melody. *Journey to the Heart: Daily Meditations on the Path to Freeing Your Soul*. San Francisco: HarperSanFrancisco, 1996.

2. Kushner, Harold S. *How Good Do We Have to Be? A New Understanding of Guilt and Forgiveness*. New York: Back Bay Books, 1996.

3. Sinek, Simon. *Start with Why*. New York: Portfolio Penguin Random House. 2011.

4. Baker, Adam. Facebook page, January 22, 2022. www.facebook.com/Adam Baker.

5. Price, Reynolds. *A Whole New Life: An Illness and a Healing*. New York: Scribner, 2000.

6. As quote by Brad Lomenick in an article titled, "Leadership Identity: Part Three." https://leadership.lifeway.com.

7. Steinbeck, John. *Travels with Charley: In Search of America*. New York: Viking Penguin, 1962.

8. Bailie, Gil. *Violence Unveiled: Humanity at the Crossroads*. Pearl River: Crossroad Publishing Company, 1995.

3

~

Maintaining a Healthy Balance

Do you seek to live a wholistic life, caring for body, mind, and spirit? Do you know the warning signs of burnout? What are your physical, mental, and spiritual disciplines?

For fifteen years, I worked as the associate to D. Elton Trueblood, as well as being the director of the Yokefellow Institute located on the campus of Earlham College in Richmond, Indiana. At the height of his writing career, Dr. Trueblood was known as the dean of American religious writers. He wrote thirty-eight books, his most famous being *The Predicament of Modern Man*, *A Place to Stand*, and *The Company of the Committed*. Dr. Trueblood died in 1994, but his writings and teachings are still as relevant today as when he was alive. When we first met, he made a lasting impression.

I was a young minister at the Friends meeting in Central City, Nebraska, when Dr. Trueblood was a dinner guest at my parents' home in Wichita, Kansas. He was in Wichita to help inaugurate the new president of Friends University, and I was there at the invitation of my parents. As we ate, Dr. Trueblood turned to me and asked, "What are you going to preach on this coming First Day?" This was Monday, and so I had not yet begun to think about a sermon for Sunday! I responded that I did not know. He said, "I want you to speak on the Holy Conjunction." I told him that I would, but I did not know what it is. He then took out his pocket Bible and turned to the Gospel of Matthew, chapter 22, when the lawyer asks Jesus, "Teacher, which is the great commandment in the Law?" Jesus answers, "You shall love the Lord your God with all your heart *and* with all your soul *and* with all your mind. This is the great and first commandment. *And* a second is like it: You shall love your neighbor as yourself" (verses 36–39; emphasis added). "The Holy Conjunction," said Dr. Trueblood, "is the word 'and.'"

I have never forgotten these words from my mentor. His important point was that the life of a Christian is a life of balance and conjunction—the combination of the clear head *and* the warm heart, the inner life of devotion *and* the outer life of ministry, the conservation of important traditions *and* the need to be open to new ideas. In the span of forty-five minutes over dinner, Dr. Trueblood initiated within me a course of thought that has continued to this day.

Life can be divided into compartments. The dissected life is the opposite of the healthy and balanced wholeness that we should seek. The religious leaders who participate in the *Sacred Chaos* seminars are, for the most part, *not* living a life of balance and conjunction. Their lives are divided into compartments, where they can be one person at home and another person at work. They have habits of self-medication that they try to hide from others. They lack authenticity, so their ministry suffers and their personal health suffers.

Larry was clear from the initial interview with the Sacred Chaos *leaders that he could no longer "live with himself." It had become increasingly clear to him that he was two separate selves—how he presented himself in ministry at the church, and who he was at home with his wife and children. He had become very resentful over his fifteen years of being a pastor. The resentment stemmed from that wicked combination of the pressures to perform, to accommodate the needs of the church 24/7, to earn an adequate living financially, and to stuff it all underneath being nice. Unfortunately, his anger exploded in situations with the people he longed to love the most. Apparently, this was a subtle and insidious process that developed over time, and he was unable to change the pattern. The only way that he felt he could cope was to change congregations. That was, however, only a short-lived strategy to disrupt the emotional cycle. He had developed two different personas—one in ministry at the church in which people were pleased with all his efforts, i.e., workaholism that had its own reinforcement, and one with his family at home in which he had grown emotionally estranged from his wife and overwhelmed by the ways that his three children were acting out their defensiveness and anger toward him. And all efforts to work to improve the relationships in his nuclear family turned out to be short-lived because he simply didn't have the emotional wherewithal to be present and to stay present for the needs of his family. He found himself so far removed from the ideals that he carried with him into his vocational calling—the importance of nurturing his own spiritual centeredness, making his family a priority in his life, keeping a sense of equilibrium regarding the various commitments—that he had come to the conclusion that his only way forward was to change career paths. He thought that if he did that, he could restore his relationships with his wife and children. He was certain that it was impossible for him to sustain the present course.*

In the chaos of their lives, religious leaders can be faced with any number of dyads that they are trying to process. A part of the journey of self-discovery for religious leaders is working their way through the various dyads that arise in chaos. *Love and intimacy:* What are these to me? How do I experience them? *Spirituality and religion:* Is my religious tradition meeting my spiritual needs? *Work and family:* How have my work and career defined who I am? How have my work and career intruded into my spiritual and family lives? *Relationship and aloneness:* How do I balance my need for both? *Thinking and feeling:* How do I make the journey from my head to my heart, or how do I balance my feelings with my thinking? *Freedom and responsibility:* How do I remain free and independent, and yet responsible for my actions in family and work? *Spouses and children:* Who am I when I no longer have a spouse or when children no longer "need" me? *Restlessness and contentment:* How do I handle my feelings of spiritual and emotional restlessness? Where do I experience contentment? *Mystery and faith:* Am I comfortable in the mystery surrounding God and my faith? *Loss and death:* How do I face and respond to the death of loved ones? How do I face my own mortality?

These and many other concerns are a part of processing the chaos we feel as we move from one emotional and spiritual place to another. Out of this grouping, there are four dyads in particular that I believe are most important in our quest for wholeness and spiritual growth. First is *relationship and aloneness.* Community is very important in the process of growing spiritually. We are meaning-seeking, social creatures. In relationships, we learn about love and care for one another. We learn also about *ourselves* in relationship. In loving and caring for others, we grow in our ability to love and care for ourselves. I believe that *much of the meaning in life, and so many of the ways that God would have us grow in love, can be found in that awkward dance between our yearning for relationship with others and the need to become our own individuated selves.* Living in the rhythm of being with others and being with oneself is to maintain that healthy balance needed to grow spiritually through chaos.

A second dyad of wholeness that needs emphasis is *thinking and feeling.* As with so many religious leaders, for most of my life I have lived primarily in my mind, or the thinking side of this dyad. In recent years, however, as I have gone through my own pain and chaos, the feeling or heart side of this dyad has become more important. In the awakening of my heart, I have learned many new lessons and traveled new paths of love and intimacy that could not be reached by the mind. "Now here is my secret; a very simple secret, indeed," we read in *The Little Prince.* "It is only with the heart that one can see rightly."[1] In the words of Blaise Pascal, "The heart has reasons that the mind knows not of."[2] This is true. For those who are more comfortable in the emotional and feeling side of life, however, it also is important to develop the mind. Balancing our love of God with both mind and heart helps us along our spiritual journey toward wholeness.

A third dyad of emphasis is *restlessness and contentment*. Senses of both restlessness and contentment are important to spiritual growth and our quest for wholeness. And, for the most part, we do not choose to be restless! The chaos we find ourselves in will agitate the restlessness, which is a by-product of pain and struggle.

Jean Adriel has written about leaving her spiritual teacher, Meher Baba: "The parting from Baba was an extremely painful one. In my farewell moments with him I was moved to thank him for all the joy and pain of my life with him, to which he replied: 'Thank me only for the pain.' Now, years later, I fully appreciate the wisdom of these words. The expression 'growing pain' is just as applicable to the spiritual life as it is to the physical, and without it no growth is possible for human creatures."[3] The last line of Adriel's description of how important pain is to growth may be overstated, but her point is well-taken. Over the years, I have learned to be thankful to God for *both* pain and restlessness, as well as the times of contentment when I can live out the lessons learned during my restless experiences.

A fourth dyad of conjunction that is important for religious leaders in their journey toward wholeness is the dyad of *mystery and faith*. If we are to know the Living God, we must learn to be comfortable in mystery.

The Christian television and radio stations of today as well as too many evangelical churches are filled with voices of certainty. Every time I happen to listen to these preachers, which, fortunately, is not very often, I think to myself, "I wish that I could be as sure about *anything* as they are about *everything*. They are trying to do the impossible, namely, to capture God by espousing certainties."

Fundamentalist certainties are to be found not just within conservative evangelical circles. This kind of one-dimensional thinking is also a part of some mainline churches. I once addressed a Presbyterian elders' meeting with the PC(USA) on the topic of church renewal. Out of the blue, one of the elders asked me, "Do you believe in the physical resurrection of Jesus?" I gave what I believed was a thoughtful answer, that Scripture has provided us with illustrations of both a physical resurrection and a spiritual resurrection, and so, much to this elder's dismay, I could not answer with certainty that I believe in a *physical* resurrection. Evidently, this was where this man drew his line of acceptability. If I could not answer his question in the affirmative, I could not be trusted to say anything that he could believe. He walked out.

I believe it was Mary Oliver who said, "Writers write to find God, but God is always in the next sentence." Chaos grows the mystery in our lives and in our search for God. In chaos, we learn that life is a shifting fault line and that there is no such thing as complete certainty.

Coupled with the idea of the Holy Conjunction and living a conjunct life, Dr. Trueblood introduced me to the idea of *loving the difficult*. It was at a convocation at Earlham College when I first heard Dr. Trueblood speak about the topic "Learn to Love the Difficult." It was an interesting lecture choice for an audience of five hundred students, young people who were reared in a society in which comfort, pleasure, and freedom from pain and difficulty have become the norm. In his clear and prophetic way, Dr. Trueblood challenged the contemporary desire to get by with doing as little as possible. He asked these students to consider the possibility of finding spiritual fulfillment in the *difficult*. His suggestions ranged far . . . from the study of what he called the "intellectual and spiritual giants" to the challenge of learning a second or third language. He emphasized the importance of a personal discipline that includes maintaining a healthy balance between the spiritual, mental, and physical disciplines of life. In our *Sacred Chaos* seminars, we encourage participants to develop a life of discipline, concentrating on these three important areas.

The Physical Disciplines:

1. Be careful as to what you eat, recognizing that what you consume directly affects how you feel. Do not overeat. Our doctors are telling us this all the time. Yet how difficult it is to break some of our bad habits, habits that we have been practicing for a lifetime. It is true: What we consume directly affects the way we feel. Learn the discipline of a good diet.
2. Exercise regularly, at least twenty minutes each day. When I was running every day, people would ask me, "Do you enjoy running?" My response was, "No, I do not enjoy the actual running. *What I enjoy is how I feel after I run!*" Twenty minutes per day is not requiring too much. Exercise. . . . It will change your life!
3. Consult with a physician routinely, getting a physical checkup at least once per year. Do not put off these regular visits to see a physician. No one is too busy to take care of one's physical health.

The Mental Disciplines:

1. Read at least one hundred pages per week in the field of religious study and spirituality, and one hundred pages per week in other disciplines.

Each week, take a trip to the local bookstore or visit Amazon to see what people are reading. What are the top ten bestsellers on the *New York Times* reading list? What is *new* in the area of religion and spirituality?

2. Join or organize a study group in which you can share your ideas and test your conclusions regarding what you have read. There is no *impression* without *expression*. The point is we learn from one another when we share ideas and possibilities with one another. A study group is different from a group of spiritual friends. A study group is primarily concerned with the sharing of ideas about what we are reading, whereas a group of spiritual friends is concerned about personal issues of wellness: physical, mental, and spiritual.

3. Attend at least one continuing education event per year to keep abreast of the new developments in the area of religious leadership. Religious leaders can learn from others. We do not know everything. In truth, the paradox of education is that the more we know, the more we realize there is to know. Leave the confines of your normal working context, and attend a continuing education event at least once each year.

The Spiritual Disciplines:

1. Sit in silent prayer and expectant waiting for at least fifteen minutes each day. This is a difficult discipline but one that reaps great spiritual rewards. For many of our *Sacred Chaos* participants, one of the most difficult parts of our seminars is to begin each morning in silent meditation. At the conclusion of one of our seminars, a United Methodist minister said in his evaluation that he just about "went crazy" having to sit in silence for that length of time. If one is in chaos, sitting in silence is difficult because in the silence we have to *confront ourselves*. Self-medication distracts us and keeps us from facing our issues.

2. Study the great spiritual models of history by reading the classics of religious devotion. So many of the great classics of devotion were written by persons who experienced chaos in their lives and shared about it in their writings. These authors offer religious leaders some signposts for their own journeys of self-discovery. One such author is Thomas R. Kelly, who wrote A *Testament of Devotion*. Kelly's experience of chaos began after his failure at Harvard University. Kelly was scheduled to defend his doctoral dissertation before a faculty committee. During his academic interrogation, he had what his son referred to as a "woozy

spell." Today we would probably diagnose Kelly's condition as some form of epilepsy. The end result was that he could not answer any of the questions asked of him, and he failed. And not only did he fail, but he was told that he had failed so miserably that he could never return to Harvard.

Those were difficult words for someone who had given his life to the pursuit of God through reason and philosophy. He left Harvard depressed, so much so that his wife thought that he may take his own life. This was in fall 1937.

In January 1938, Kelly, who retained his teaching position at Haverford College in Philadelphia even after the failure at Harvard, was scheduled to deliver a series of lectures at Germantown Friends Meeting in a suburb of Philadelphia. As he spoke, his words were surrounded by the authority of one who had experienced, in a transformational way, the living God. This is how he began his first lecture:

> To you in this room who are seekers, to you, young and old who have toiled all night and caught nothing, but who want to launch out into the deeps and let down your nets for a draught, I want to speak as simply, as tenderly, as clearly as I can. For God can be found. There is a last rock for your souls, a resting place of absolute peace and joy and power and radiance and security. There is a Divine Center into which your life can slip, a new and absolute orientation in God, a Center where you live with God and out of which you see all of life, through new and radiant vision, tinged with new sorrows and pangs, new joys unspeakable and full of glory.[4]

In his chaos, Kelly moved from mere knowledge about the God of history to acquaintance with the God of the immediate present. His tears of transformation began to flow after his failure at Harvard. His failure, however, made him vulnerable to a change that was wrought within the very foundation of his soul. And because of this transformation, a classic of religious devotion was born, and signposts for our own journeys were given to us.

3. Consciously work at avoiding those things, both inward and outward, that inhibit your relationship with God. One of those outward things that can inhibit our relationship with God is the cell phone. Today's religious leader is vulnerable 24/7 because his or her congregants can text and email any time of the day or night. And because communication can be so instantaneous, messages that come to the religious leader come without the benefit of *filtering*. The raw message that rarely has

been carefully thought through can be very disruptive to our mental and spiritual beings. A friend of mine recently had to tell someone to quit emailing him about the business of the church, business that should come before the church board. He wrote, "Your emails have been emotionally upsetting for me. I think I am doing the work of the church, and then I get blindsided by your messages. It is emotionally jarring, leading me into a negative spiral of alternating regret, recrimination, resentment and so on. . . . Your concerns need to be brought forward at the appropriate time, and that is the board meeting." Religious leaders can discipline themselves to turn the phone off, especially if they are constantly being bothered by disgruntled congregants.

Outward things like the cell phone and television can be disruptive to one's leadership and spiritual growth. We can, however, discipline ourselves to turn them off. A more difficult problem is turning off the negative inner issues that stunt our leadership and growth in spirit. One of the more common issues for religious leaders is cynicism and negative criticism that often erupts at inappropriate times and with persons who are not responsible for the negativity. Criticism of others and put-downs that wound the hearts of others can be self-destructive of our own spirits.

4. Invite two friends to meet with you weekly in a spiritual support group in which you can openly share your personal cares and concerns, without fear of ridicule or breach of trust. Again, religious leaders need spiritual friendships in which they can be authentic, sharing what is going on in their lives and finding encouraging voices to help them through difficult issues. Wherever I am in my ministry, I seek out those friends who can be trusted with my issues and who will not be judgmental of the life choices I have made. The key ingredient to any such relationship is *trust*.

Keeping these disciplines can be hard work, but by doing so, we will be able to add more positive ways in which we can work toward living a balanced and wholistic life.

Three other ways by which we can do this . . .

1. *The "Full" Datebook.* Whether you use your phone or still use a paper calendar, each January 1, take some time to mark out days and weeks for the year ahead when you will take time for yourself. These are times when you are not available to others. If someone calls and wants to set

up a time to see you or plan a meeting during these times, it is easy to say, "I am unavailable." The reason you are unavailable is because you have an appointment with yourself. Also, be sure to cross out times for continuing education events and times for spiritual retreat.

2. *Simmering Walks.* It was Howard Thurman who wrote, "Our spirits resound with clashings, while something deep within hungers and thirsts for the still moment and resting lull."[5] I love the word "simmering." It is a word born out of meditative silence but has more to do with life rhythm than with lack of sound. Something about the word reaches deep into my soul. This is especially true when words like "frantic," "hurry," and "impatience" describe the experiences through which I have just passed. "Simmering" is a calming word, a word closely associated with, if not synonymous with, "lingering" and "savoring."

When I was a younger man, I was a long-distance runner. These days I am a long-distance walker. I miss my days of running, but walking has given me much-needed times for simmering. *Simmering walks*, as I have come to call them, are wonderful opportunities to reflect on the day's activities and my relational encounters. Some queries I ask myself as I walk include: "Am I using the sacred gift of time today in a meaningful way?" "Have I been helpful in lifting human burdens today?" "Have I been an encourager to those who are in need of encouragement?" "What spiritual lessons am I learning from today's experiences?" As I walk, I think of those I love and pray for them. I also think of those who need that element of extra grace and who can be especially difficult and de-energizing, and pray for them as well. On occasion, I physically lift my arms and wrap certain persons in God's light.

3. *Gratitude Journals.* On NPR's *Morning Edition*, there was a segment titled "If You Feel Thankful, Write It Down. It's Good For Your Health." The report said, "There's a growing body of research on the benefits of gratitude. Studies have found that giving thanks and counting blessings can help people sleep better, lower stress and improve interpersonal relationships." As an example, the report shared about a mental health counselor who had lost her job and was sleeping on her friend's mom's couch. "She felt like she was reaching for reasons to be grateful . . . but she still tried to find some. . . . Ultimately it helped. 'It allowed me to ground myself,' she says. 'It allowed me to remember what was going well in a world full of chaos.'"[6]

To maintain a healthy and balanced perspective on the world, one's family, and one's ministry, the religious leader can offset the feelings of chaos with gratitude for those things that are "going well." Keeping a *gratitude journal* can help one do that.

The internet is filled with articles and suggestions for the self-care of religious leaders, and since the pandemic, there have been many new issues which the religious leader has been forced to deal with. The stress among religious leaders today is enormous, and the participants in the *Sacred Chaos* seminars bear this out. The most recent statistic shows that around 1,500 religious leaders leave or retire from the ministry each month.[7] This exit from the religious institution has accelerated since the pandemic, and the rise of distrust of people in authority within congregations is increasing at a rapid pace. Caroline is a good example of one who has left the religious institution under stress.

Caroline went to seminary in her late forties, after her three children had all graduated from high school. She and her husband divorced approximately ten years ago. The time seemed to be right for her to respond to a long-standing sense of being called to love and serve God's people. Though she certainly had developed people skills as a real-estate agent, even seminary did not prepare her for the challenges of serving three small rural churches with a variety of expectations, considerable driving, family-oriented controlling behaviors, and all the churches competing for her time, energy, and attention. Two issues became apparent, which she brought with her to the Sacred Chaos *seminar: 1) She was having considerable difficulties saying no and managing her time. She was becoming exhausted. And 2) She found it shocking just how critical parishioners could be in getting what they needed and wanted from their pastor. She recognized her need to be assertive—clear and direct, but also gracious and compassionate. When she arrived at* Sacred Chaos, *she was disappointed that she was not yet able to make gains in this direction.*

Working to live a wholistic life is a full-time undertaking. The institutions that we religious leaders serve will not do this for us. The people *within* the institutions can love the religious leaders and care for their well-being, but the institution itself, with all its survival mechanisms in place, *cannot.* Institutions are institutions because they will live on long after we have gone. They have a fierce survivalist mentality complete with congregational leaders, guidebooks, endowments, and traditions. In fact, the rewards are great for *not* taking care of oneself and becoming a workaholic for the institution.

When I was serving on the faculty of a school of religion, my dean lived right across the street from my corner office. He would take great delight in telling the board of trustees how hard the faculty worked and would often use me as an example. "I see Jim's light on in his office late into the night, where he is writing and preparing for a class." Institutions and their leadership love the workaholic. Of course, the truth was I was having difficulty in my marriage and family life, and so I medicated myself by working late hours. *I was burning out.* And this is not uncommon for those serving religious institutions.

When I was the director of the Yokefellow Institute, an ecumenical center for retreats and continuing education primarily for religious leaders, I would often lead conferences for clergy. One particular gathering stands out for the openness and honesty with which these pastors talked about the chaos into which they had been thrown as a result of the emotional and spiritual fatigue in their lives. As they gathered in the meeting room, they seemed to be genuinely enjoying one another's company. The program's focus for the next few days was to be stress in the ministry, and the quiet and peaceful surroundings of the back campus of Earlham College were already providing a healing influence on the conference attendees. As we sat together in that beautiful room overlooking the rolling hills of central Indiana, the participants began to share how they were feeling about their ministries, both spiritually and emotionally. Since it was an interdenominational group and the participants had not known one another before they arrived, there was considerable freedom to be honest about what they were feeling in their work.

One by one, these ministers began to share their life stories—their calls to ministry, the churches they had served, and how they were feeling now. What soon became the operative word for this session together was "burnout." All had been pastors long enough to feel the frustration and know the difficulties of serving a local congregation. For the most part, these were "mainline" pastors who were experiencing the pressures of the last few decades of both numerical and financial decline, as well as the other cultural and societal pressures all pastors are feeling as they seek to do ministry in a chaotic world. Some were ready to leave the ministry for other work; some were looking for new pastorates, hoping that a change in geography would boost their sagging spirits; and some were just going to *tough it out* until retirement. All were spiritually and emotionally tired.

Burnout in ministry is on the rise. All of the religious leaders who come to our *Sacred Chaos* seminars either are burned out or are on the verge of burnout. The Mayo Clinic has recognized the problem of burnout throughout our society and has shared some observations. Here is what the clinic lists as some symptoms of burnout, putting them in question form: *Have you become cynical or critical at work? Do you drag yourself to work and have trouble getting started? Have you become irritable or impatient with coworkers? Do you lack the energy to be consistently productive? Do you find it hard to concentrate?*

Do you lack satisfaction from your achievements? Do you feel disillusioned about your work? Are you using drugs or alcohol to feel better or to simply not feel? Have your sleep habits changed? Are you troubled by unexplained headaches, stomach or bowel problems, or other physical complaints?[8]

Burnout is more than just stress. It is *chronic* stress that can lead to physical and emotional exhaustion, cynicism, avoidance of connection with others, and a feeling of ineffectiveness in one's ministry. "What's the use?" is a common expression for those in the throes of burnout. In the words of a colleague, "Burnout is when the hamster is lying dead in the cage, but the hamster wheel continues to spin!"

Burnout can be prevented by recognizing that *our inner lives need to be continuously nurtured.* We cannot be confronting the world all the time, 24/7. We can learn a great deal about the nurturing of our inner lives by the example of Jesus. Throughout the Gospels, we discover a pattern of encounter with the world and then withdrawal from the world for spiritual revitalization. What becomes apparent from reading about the life of Jesus is that he understood his effectiveness in the world to be directly related to his spiritual condition. The examples are numerous: "And after he had dismissed the crowds, he went up on the mountain by himself to pray" (Matthew 14:23). "And rising very early in the morning, while it was still dark, he departed and went out to a desolate place, and there he prayed" (Mark 1:35). "Perceiving then that they were about to come and take him by force to make him king, Jesus withdrew again to the mountain by himself" (John 6:15). "But now even more the report about him went abroad, and great crowds gathered to hear him and to be healed of their infirmities. But he would withdraw to desolate places and pray" (Luke 5:15–16).

This last text is especially meaningful for religious leaders for it shows that when Jesus was needed most, he would "withdraw to desolate places."

Although much has changed since the time of Jesus, the human condition is still basically the same. The encounters with the world, if anything, have increased. What is needed is a contemporary understanding of "wilderness."

Steve came to our *Sacred Chaos* seminar openly admitting that he felt burned out. He was ready to leave the ministry as well as his wife and family. Nothing that he had tried could get him to shake the feeling of chaos.

Steve was now almost sixty years old and was just trying to get to retirement. He was emotionally tired, spiritually weary, physically worn out, fresh out of ideas, and exhausted in his efforts to keep up with the ever-changing demands of technology. He admitted that the only motivation he still had was that he had only six more years of ministry to maximize the financial picture for his retirement. It did not help that he was starting to have some chronic health issues, such as being overweight with type 2 diabetes, high cholesterol with a heart condition, and bad knees, which had caught up with him from playing football back in high school. He recognized that he was not taking care of himself. He felt trapped professionally and stuck in a rut, and was apparently quite depressed. His physician had recently prescribed an antidepressant. And so, burned out, Steve was limping his way toward retirement. His only hope was that his retirement would bring a more enjoyable quality of life.

In the vulnerability of such burnout and chaos, we can become ever more conscious of the greatest of human adventures . . . *spiritual growth.* In our quest for wholeness, in recognizing the importance of the Holy Conjunction "and," our lives can find an exit to the spiritually destructive spiral of a compartmentalized and dissected existence that keeps us in chaos. The important counsel for religious leaders in chaos is the good news that the chaos does not have to last forever. "I saw also that there was an ocean of darkness and death, but an infinite ocean of light and love, which flowed over the ocean of darkness," wrote George Fox in his *Journal.*[9] It is in this "ocean of light and love" that we place our faith and our hope.

Notes

1. Saint-Exupéry, Antoine de. *The Little Prince.* Translated by Alan Wakeman. Herefordshire: Wordsworth Classics, 1995.

2. Pascal, Blaise. *Pensées.* Translated by A. J. Krailsheimer. New York: Penguin Classics, 1995.

3. Mount, Meher. "Thank You For All The Joy And Pain In My Life." Meher Mount Corporation, October 28, 2015. https://www.mehermount.org/story-blog/2015/10/2810/tthankful-for-suffering.

4. Kelly, Thomas R. *A Testament of Devotion.* New York: Harper and Brothers, 1941.

5. Thurman, Howard. *Meditations of the Heart.* Boston: Beacon Press, 1999.

6. National Public Radio Report, *Morning Edition.* Uroda, Kristen. "If You Feel Thankful, Write It Down. It's Good For Your Health." December 24, 2018.

7. Pastoral Care, Inc. "Statistics in the Minstry," 2020. https://pastoralcareinc.com/statistics.

8. Mayo Clinic. "Job burnout: How to spot it and take action." June 5, 2021. www.mayoclinic.org.

9. Fox, George. *The Journal of George Fox.* Edited by John Nickalls. Philadelphia: Philadelphia Yearly Meeting, 1997.

4

⟿

Power, Control, and Heart-Centered Leadership

Have the issues of power and control, the lure of materialism, and the hunger for prestige interfered with the effectiveness of your ministry? How has chaos moved you to a more heart-centered ministry? Do you understand the servant-leadership model?

It was Thomas Kelly who wrote, "Within the silences of the souls of persons an eternal drama is ever being enacted, in these days as well as in others. And *on the outcome of this inner drama rests, ultimately, the outer pageant of history*"[1] (italics added). These words from Kelly were written during World War II. Even in the middle of one of the greatest world calamities of the twentieth century, Kelly had the insight and experience of God within his own heart to recognize that the outer pageant of history is dependent upon how each of us deals with the inner drama taking place within our souls.

I have been thinking about my father in recent days and the inner drama that went on within him. He was the personification of what you would call a successful minister. He put the church he served and his community and fellow humans above himself. Unfortunately, there were many times he put others above his own family. His statement "I am married to the church" was one that I would hear often during my growing years, and one that was deeply hurtful to my mother.

In an editorial in the *Star* newspaper in Muncie, Indiana, printed on the day of my father's memorial service, the editor of the paper wrote about my father. He said, "Newby died last week at the comparatively young age of 62, yet his record of accomplishments is long and distinguished. He accumulated that record by never flinching from accepting responsibility, regardless of whether the request was from his church, community, or from the downtrodden and less fortunate who sought his counsel and friendship. . . . He was a thoughtful and inspiring speaker. His sermons were carefully researched and meticulous in their preparation. Two published volumes of those sermons remain as his legacy. . . . Also part of that legacy is the affection he engendered in those who knew him and the respect in which he was held by his church community. No person can expect more than that."[2]

My father was a Quaker minister and a Quaker pacifist, never flinching from his heartfelt belief that Jesus was right when he taught his followers to "love your enemies." He was a conscientious objector during World War II, which was a courageous position to take in those days, often resulting in him being ostracized or beaten by those who disagreed with his position. He was a man who as a child experienced near death as a result of scarlet fever and rheumatic fever. He would tell the story of being in his bed sick and hearing the doctor outside the room telling his mother to prepare for his death. And yet he survived, for which I am personally grateful!

The spirituality of remembrance . . . The stories, the memories and pictures in the mind are all there. I am sure that I am a Quaker minister because of my father's influence. There came a time in my life, however, when I began to see that many of the destructive patterns of my father's life were also finding expression within me. Yes, he was "successful" according to the standards of the world. Yes, he was "married to the church" and he lived this truth out every day of his short life. As the editorial about him stated, his "record of accomplishments is long and distinguished. He accumulated that record by never flinching from responsibility." And finally, his workaholism and his sense of commitment and duty to the church he married shortened his life. Toward the end, I remember talking to my father about his life and ministry. He spoke about the growth of fundamentalism within the orthodox branch of Quakerism, a truth that greatly upset him. There was a feeling of futility in his speech, a feeling that for all he had done to advance the cause of civil rights and progressive concern for what he called "man's inhumanity to man," it was all for naught. I also sensed in him some growth in movement from his head to his heart, which was verified for me at his memorial service.

The meeting room at Friends Memorial Church in Muncie, Indiana was full to overflowing. Many persons from the various spheres of my father's life were there to pay their final respects to this minister and community leader. Both the current Democratic mayor and the former Republican mayor were there, as were the president of Earlham College and numerous business leaders. During the time of silent reflection, when persons were given the opportunity to say a few words about my father, many stood and reflected upon his life of ministry and social activism. Today I cannot recall what any of them said. *I do remember*, however, what one little fellow wearing glasses said who was enrolled in the Friends Preschool at Friends Memorial. He walked up to the front of the meeting room and said in a bold and confident voice, "Richard Newby was my friend!" I later learned that my father had a special interest in and concern for the children in the preschool who wore glasses. My father had worn glasses from the age of four to the day he died, and he understood the cruel remarks that children who wear glasses have to endure. His heart hurt for them, and he became their friend.

When he died, I believe that he was in a time of chaos in his life, a chaos that he did not know how to grow out of. And before he could adequately work through his issues, both personal and those related to the communities of faith he served, he died. I have wondered how my father would have reacted to what is going on in our world today, this world filled with tension and anxiety in which *new* strains of COVID-19 are constantly being found, and inflation and gas prices are on the rise, and the divisions within the political realm are becoming more and more accentuated, and the church is in a frantic search for relevancy. How would the inner drama about which Kelly wrote be played out within him? More importantly for us today, how is this drama being played out within *us*, who are living through it?

When religious leaders find themselves in chaos, one of the first internal adjustments to be made is how they understand themselves and how this understanding is reflected in their leadership. Those who come to the *Sacred Chaos* seminars are usually at a place where the old leadership ways do not work anymore . . . not for them or for the congregations they serve. In brief, religious leaders in chaos find themselves having to come to terms with the drama that is going on inside of them, as well as the changing dynamics of local congregations trying to remain relevant in a changing world. And some of the major issues associated with this drama are the issues of *power and control, the lure of materialism, and the hunger for prestige.*

If we turn to the Bible and other spiritual literature, we learn that those who wrote these writings had an understanding of power that is fundamentally different from the world's understanding of power. The world worships the power of dominance, control, prestige, status, influence, money, and achievement. It talks about power in terms of armaments, and the most powerful nation being the one with the most missiles and bombs. In 2021 the United States spent $750 billion on what is called "defense," a figure that should concern any Christian who claims to follow a man who said, "Love your enemies." The symbols of God's power, however, are different. Jesus talked about loving our neighbors as ourselves, and how the last will be first and the first will be last. He talked about things that rub the edges of our fears and insecurities. He talked about loving the least powerful and the most despised—sinners, traitors, prostitutes, and tax collectors. He treated the shamed with honor and declared the unclean clean. All of this he could do because he understood the hard task of love and did not fall for the easy substitute of worldly power. In the upside-down world of values that Jesus professed, Jesus would want us to choose *love over power*.

The worldly expressions of power can be hard for religious leaders to resist. I have sadly watched many clergy succumb to the lure of worldly power. Money, prestige, and influence in the powerful circles of government have been a huge temptation to these ministers of the Gospel. Called to be a servant to one who called himself a servant, many ministers of the Gospel have become the *served*.

A large church in the South invited me to deliver a series of lectures during the season of Lent. On Sunday, the conclusion of my time with them, I spoke at the early worship service and again later in the morning at the more formal eleven-o'clock service. Between worship services, the senior minister invited me to his study. Sitting beside his desk, the minister buzzed his personal servant and asked him to bring us some coffee. Within five minutes, the minister's butler, complete with a white jacket, appeared in the study with a silver tray and cups of coffee. The minister dismissed the butler by saying, "That will be all." Bowing politely, the butler backed out of the study. It was an amazing experience, and one that I do not normally have when I am invited to be a guest speaker. Usually someone shows me where the Styrofoam cups are located and points me in the direction of the coffee maker!

It is easy to enjoy such worldly comforts, and it is easy to succumb to the temptations of worldly power. I remember an interview I conducted with former *Punch* magazine editor and BBC commentator Malcolm Muggeridge. He was a writer and journalist, a "vendor of words," he would call himself. Late in life, Muggeridge converted to Christianity, largely due to the influence of Mother Teresa, whom he interviewed for a BBC documentary titled *Something Beautiful for God*. In the course of our interview, I asked him, "What recent developments within the Christian movement cause you the greatest concern?" He said, "The only way that you can really destroy the Christian faith is to abolish the word of our Lord, specifically when he said that his Kingdom is not of this world, and then try to prove that it is. And this is what is happening in the Christian Church today."[3]

"I am among you as the one who serves," said Jesus (Luke 22:27). *This is the most radical sentence in the world,* and one which religious leaders need to take to heart. In light of this sentence, and with the backdrop of the concern of Malcolm Muggeridge, "What is preventing us from embracing the upside-down world of values that Jesus taught and the Kingdom for which he longed?" There are many things that prevent me, a religious leader, from such an embrace, and I know that I am not alone. To live out one's faith and spirituality in the midst of this physical world is very difficult. And it is difficult because of the inner drama that is going on within us between the values that Jesus espouses and the values of this world. This drama is being played out as an *inner tug-of-war*, and is often a part of the chaos that our *Sacred Chaos* participants experience.

When Robert arrived at the Sacred Chaos *seminar, he was ready to resign from ministry altogether. He had two emotionally distressful matters with which he had struggled for years. Now, in his mid-forties after twenty years of serving as a pastor to three different congregations, he could not see a way forward past a personal issue and past a church-leadership issue. Both of these challenges created in him an inner spiritual and emotional conflict between the values of the reign of God as understood in the life and teachings of Jesus and his current, unrelenting problematic behaviors. At the personal level, Robert was unsuccessful again and again at stopping his addiction to pornography, succumbing more recently through the availability of pornography on the internet. Robert seemed to have a tremendous amount of guilt and consequent anxiety about these compulsive behaviors, and yet they provided him with temporary relief from painful emotions. At the professional level, he had a tremendous amount of angst over what was required of him each year for the stewardship campaign—to keep the church solvent in all its ministries. Though he tried again and again to make this endeavor a spiritual matter, he found himself compromising the values of Jesus in two ways: 1) Each year, it seemed, there was more and more guilt used to make the budget, and 2) There was more and more avoidance of addressing the hard issues in his sermons, particularly any prophetic message on racial injustices, so as not to offend certain members in the congregation who were big financial contributors. This caused a dichotomy that Robert was no longer able to wrap his head and heart around. It was simply too much. He felt shameful about his use of pornography, and he felt guilty over his abandonment and compromise of the values of Jesus in his work at the church. Even though he cited Paul's description of such struggles in Romans 7:15, "I do not understand my own actions. For I do not do what I want, but I do the very thing I hate," he unfortunately could not find a way to embrace the grace necessary to bring about redemptive changes over which he felt such guilt.*

The lure of materialism in North America is a direct affront to the values taught by Jesus and those which caused Robert such distress during the annual stewardship campaign at his church. To state a truism, we are living in a culture of abundance. With advertising becoming more and more important in our lives, we are enticed constantly to purchase the latest gadget or the newest version of _____ (fill in the blank). America's philosophical credo could be, "I buy, therefore I am."

The writings of John Woolman, particularly his *Journal* and essay "A Plea for the Poor," have been very important in my spiritual life. (See the epilogue, "A Model of Spirituality in a Time of Tribalism and Chaos.") This eighteenth-century Quaker struggled with his own desires in business and making money, and the effect that such business had on his inner life. He writes in his *Journal* about this struggle: "The increase of business became my burden," he says, "for though my natural inclination was towards merchandising, yet I believed that Truth required me to live more free from outward cumbers. . . . *I then lessened my outward business*"[4] (italics added). How easy Woolman makes this sound! We all have a natural inclination toward the material, including religious leaders. And yet, when an affluent society would have us believe that happiness consists in the type of car we drive or the size of the home in which we live, the upside-down world of Jesus, specifically in his statement that we find in the Gospel of Luke, reminds us, "One's life does not consist in the abundance of his possessions" (Luke 12:15).

Another aspect associated with the lure of worldly power and control and the temptations of materialism is *the hunger for prestige*. This is especially common within religious leadership circles, primarily because there is so little prestige associated with being a religious leader as well as the insecurity so many feel. If we were to trust the media for its depictions of religious leadership, we would find ourselves portrayed as either Elmer Gantry–type characters or Father Mulcahys from the TV series *M.A.S.H.* One is lacking any ethics . . . a charlatan . . . and the other is one who has little purpose, a mere appendage to an army unit who has no real influence on the personnel around him.

The human capacity for vain glory is enormous. Forever seeking recognition and approval, and in search of ways to feed our egos, religious leaders can go through life in a continuous state of aggravation. I like the humor found in the church sign that read, "This Sunday, the Reverend Doctor Jones speaking, MDiv, DD, PhD, LLD, topic, *humility*."

The African American theologian Howard Thurman is one of my spiritual heroes. Thurman would conclude his sermons by saying, "I don't know . . . I don't know . . . It may be." In closing his messages in this way, Thurman left his hearers with much to contemplate. Long after the thoughts in his sermons were forgotten, the depth of the speaker's *humility* would be remembered. *It may be . . .*

Humility. It is a spiritual quality that we could use more of these days. We are living in a time when more and more people seem more and more certain of their opinions and beliefs. Apparently, many persons think the more often and the more loudly that they proclaim their beliefs, the more their hearers will be convinced of those beliefs' truth. Raising questions, looking at possible exceptions, or maintaining a healthy level of doubt toward one's assumptions are rarely evident in today's public discourse. What is causing this wave of certitude?

Religious leaders are persons who are giving their lives to the formation and development of community, and right now they are finding themselves living in a hyper-individualistic time. The good of the individual, it is believed by many, exceeds concern for the good of the many. The whole debate over vaccinations is a good illustration of the focus that many have on individual rights. We also see this argument over gun ownership. How many mass shootings by unstable people does a society tolerate before it reexamines the Second Amendment to the Constitution? Within the realm of the faith community, this focus on individualism means giving priority to individual spiritual needs over the needs and mission of the religious community. Many Americans view their religious involvement in church, synagogue, or mosque as a journey among individuals rather than a community moving together.

Many factors directly or indirectly contribute to this focus on individualism. One is certainly the fragmentation of the family. With both parents in a household working, and children involved in everything from soccer and music lessons to the latest martial arts and tennis programs, modern families are run ragged. There is not enough time during the week to complete all the work that needs to be done, so the weekend becomes a time of picking up after the week just passed and preparing for the week to come. Although Sunday morning is still the traditional time for most Americans to attend worship in a faith community, the competition for those two hours is constantly increasing.

I remember reading an article from *TIME* magazine many years ago titled "How America Has Run Out of Time." The article is not dated! In fact, the *time crunch* increases daily. One of the fastest-growing industries today is the service industry, and the service that does it faster wins the business. Ready-to-prepare meals that are home-delivered, as well as someone else doing your grocery shopping, are just two examples of the new time-saving industry. This *time crunch* fosters individualism, as it permits less opportunity for the building of community within the family structure or the family within the faith community.

As we have become less and less involved in one another's lives, which has been accentuated by the pandemic, we have become more and more isolated as a people. This, I believe, is one of the reasons we have such a *cacophony of certitudes*. A loving and diverse society and community would challenge our certitudes. We need one another to help check and balance our belief systems as well as the certitudes we express. Anna Quindlen wrote an article titled "Life of the Closed Mind" in which she ponders, "Is that true? Maybe I should change my mind? When was the last time you can remember a public dialogue that followed that useful discourse?"[5] How different this is from the individualistic sentiment I saw expressed on a bumper sticker on the back of a pickup truck, a truck that was flying both a Confederate flag and a "Trump for President" flag. It read, "I don't give a f___ what you believe!"

The columnist George Will expresses well the need for the spiritual virtue of humility in all our discourse. He writes, "America is currently awash in an unpleasant surplus of clanging, clashing certitudes. It has been well said that the spirit of liberty is the spirit of not being too sure that you are right. One way to immunize ourselves against misplaced certitude is to contemplate, even savor, the strangeness of everything, including ourselves."[6]

In the Bible, the heart is a metaphor for the inner self. Our inner dramas, in which we are dealing with the issues of power and control, the lure of materialism, and the hunger for prestige, are being played out, according to Scripture, within our "hearts." When our hearts are awakened, our inner being, our inner self connects with the Inner Light or the Living God.

For some time now, we have witnessed examples of what happens when closed hearts and open hearts clash. This clash is taking place over interpretations of Scripture, the issues of immigration, racial justice, the inequality in the distribution of wealth, marriage equality, the ordination of gay clergy, gender identity, as well as all the issues surrounding the pandemic (masks or no masks . . . vaccinations or no vaccinations) and abortion. Before we can discuss the awakened heart, it is important to understand what it means to have a *closed* heart. What goes with a closed heart? What is that condition like?

I am grateful to the late theologian and author Marcus Borg for many things, but I am most grateful for his two books *Meeting Jesus Again for the First Time* and *The Heart of Christianity*. It is in *The Heart of Christianity* that Borg describes what a closed heart looks like. He says, first, that *a closed heart affects the mind and the reasoning process itself*. Persons with closed hearts are able to believe their own deceptions and rationalize their self-interest and narcissism.

Second, Borg says that *a closed heart and bondage go together*. We can be in bondage to all those things that our hearts desire, whether it is bondage to wealth, power, or fame.

Third, he says *a closed heart lacks gratitude*. If successful in life, or what our society holds up as successful, a person with a closed heart often feels self-made and entitled. Or, if life has gone badly, bitter and cheated. Gratitude cannot enter a heart that is bitter or that feels entitled.

Fourth, *a closed heart is insensitive to wonder and awe*. When our hearts are closed, the world looks ordinary and we are not impressed with the beauty of the natural world.

Fifth, *a closed heart forgets God*. It does not remember the one in whom we live and move and have our being. It loses track of the *mystery* that is always around us.

Sixth, *a closed heart and exile go together*. Self-preoccupied, turned inward upon itself, the shut heart is cut off from a larger reality. Separated and disconnected, it is estranged from reality and in exile.

Seventh, *a closed heart lacks compassion*. In the Bible, compassion is the ability to feel the feelings of another and then act accordingly. A closed heart does not feel this. . . . A closed heart does not feel the suffering of others.

There is a political commercial running in the state where I reside. It is about a young man who wants to be a United States senator. He is standing under a bridge with the slogan "I am a pro-Trump legal immigrant." This commercial is filled with lies as he spews forth his hatred toward immigrants, showing brown people trying to cross the border into the United States. I find myself muting the commercial whenever it comes on, and it comes on a lot! I have wondered as I have watched the words come out of his mouth, "What has happened in this man's life that he has such vitriol toward persons seeking a better life for themselves and their families?" Rather than showing us some positive steps on how our immigration policy can be fixed, his response is to build a taller wall. As Robert Frost muses, "Before I built a wall I'd ask to know / What I was walling in or walling out, / And to whom I was like to give offense. / Something there is that doesn't love a wall."[7]

Finally, says Borg, *a closed heart is insensitive to injustice*. Closed hearts and injustice go together.

Hardened hearts or closed hearts are associated with all those things that Jesus taught against . . . brutality, arrogance, greed, not welcoming the stranger, mistreatment of the poor, violence, etc. Milder forms of a hardened heart can even find their way into the communal life of a congregation, such as being judgmental, insensitive, and self-righteous.[8]

How do we lead from the perspective of an awakened heart? How do we nurture those places where the sacred and the self connect and the heart is awakened? What are those marks that go with an open or awakened heart?

A few years ago, I facilitated a grant from the Lilly Endowment that supported a program that became known as NET Groups. NET is an acronym for *Nurturing Experience Theologically*. It was designed to offer an alternative to religious education programs that focused on *information* as opposed to *transformation*. This program is fully described in the book *Gathering the Seekers*, which I published through the Alban Institute.[9] While sharing how this program works, I offer some descriptive words about the kind of persons who would be attracted to such a program. These are also some of the marks of a religious leader who has been through chaos and is now leading out of an awakened heart.

An awakened heart is an open heart . . . open to new ideas . . . open to new ways of ministry . . . open to new relationships and open to being surprised by the leading of the Spirit within oneself. Leading from the heart requires us to be open and to believe in the continuing revelation of God.

An awakened heart is also a heart that is nonjudgmental. A judgmental heart is negative and discouraging. A nonjudgmental heart is encouraging and supportive of congregants, regardless of place along the spiritual-growth continuum. Religious leaders need close spiritual friends to remind them when they slip into a cynical and judgmental posture.

An awakened heart is a seeking heart. This mark is closely associated with the mark of being open but adds the element of *active search*. How is God at work in my experiences? What spiritual lessons am I learning? A seeking heart wants to learn about new ideas and new approaches to spiritual growth. Seeking and an awakened heart go together.

An awakened heart is also a questioning heart. Throughout my life, I have been encouraged to ask questions. "Why?" has been a continuous refrain in my time on this earth. "But how?" and "What if?" have filled the spaces in between. Despite the inherent expectation of an answer to each question asked, I have found that in the tension between the asking of the question and the receiving of the answer, there is the greatest possibility for understanding. As in most profound educational and spiritual adventures, wisdom does not come in the answer, whatever it may be, but in asking the question. In an article for *Spirituality and Health* magazine, Sam Keen notes, "What you ask is who you are" and "what shapes our lives are questions we ask, refuse to ask, or never think of asking."[10]

An awakened heart is a compassionate heart. Religious leaders, by and large, are a very caring group of folks. They feel the pain that others are going through, and they respond with the best tools that they have to try to alleviate the pain.

A friend of mine was in the middle of an elders' meeting at his church and he felt led to share about the difficulty that he was having with one of the congregation's members. The member was a classic closed-heart kind of fellow, and my friend was having a really difficult time relating to him, especially after this member verbally assaulted him. One of the elders responded to my friend's concern by saying, "You just have to develop a tougher skin." To this my friend said, "Is that what this church wants? A minister with a 'tough skin'?" A compassionate religious leader does not have a tough skin. He or she feels what is going on within the lives of persons in the congregation and seeks to help. This help, however, has boundaries, and the minister needs to take care of himself or herself if being verbally abused.

An awakened heart is also a heart that is self-aware. Self-awareness means that the religious leader is aware of his or her traits, behaviors, and feelings. On the website My Question Life, there is this definition: "Self-awareness is our ability to notice our thoughts and feelings and how they influence our behaviors. . . . At its core, self-awareness is our ability to understand ourselves and how we fit into the world."[11] When religious leaders are self-aware, their personal relationships are strengthened, and their ability to relate to the congregations they serve is enhanced.

An awakened heart is also a heart that has a passion for justice. This passion for justice finds expression in a radical love that leads to actions for justice that are risky and challenge many of society's norms. A radical love and passion for justice will question the vast sums of money that our government spends on wars, past, present, and future. Such love will question the humanity of an immigration system that punishes rather than encourages persons coming to America seeking a better life. A passion for justice embraces diversity in all its beauty: diversity in race, class, gender, and sexual orientation. This kind of radical love is born in the chaos through which the religious leader has traveled. And it does not just happen. Religious leaders have choices. We can decide that the life we are living and the leadership that we are expressing in keeping things as they are is as good as it can get, or we can see and understand life and leadership through the lens of radical love that embraces a passion for justice. This means seeing through the myriad of unloving distractions that are obstructing our sight and limiting us spiritually and emotionally. It means becoming instruments of the prophetic task of the church, which theologian and Hebrew Scripture scholar Walter Brueggemann describes as "telling the truth in a society that lives in illusion, grieving in a society that practices denial, and expressing hope in a society that lives in despair."[12] And my good friend Professor Clarence White would add to these prophetic tasks "poking holes in false narratives!" Former Archbishop of El Salvador Óscar Romero challenges the church and offers an explanation for why he was assassinated with these words: "A church that doesn't provoke any crises, a gospel that doesn't unsettle, a word of God that doesn't get under any one's skin, a word of God that doesn't touch the real sin of the society in which it is being proclaimed—What gospel is that?" A passion for justice that is fueled by a radical love is a part of an awakened heart.

A religious leader who leads from an awakened heart carries within this heart these seven qualities: *openness, a nonjudgmental spirit, a seeking spirit, a questioning spirit, compassion for others, self-awareness, and a passion for justice.* Many of these qualities also are part of what it means to be described as a *servant leader.*

The idea of *servant leadership* is the brainchild of Robert K. Greenleaf, who coined the term in his 1970 essay "The Servant as Leader." What he describes as a *servant leader* fits very well with how we believe religious leaders should lead. In an article titled "Character and Servant Leadership: 10 Characteristics of Effective, Caring Leaders," which was published in *The Journal of Virtues and Leadership*, Larry Spears, former president of the Robert K. Greenleaf Center for Servant Leadership, lists what he considers the ten most important characteristics of servant leaders.

1. *Listening.* Religious leaders can be so busy that they can lose their listening skills. The servant leader knows how to listen to people, focusing with full attention on what is being said.
2. *Empathy.* A servant leader is a caring leader. A servant leader can feel the pain of others and responds to others with heartfelt love and support.
3. *Healing.* A servant leader in a religious community strives to make the community a place of healing for those who enter it. If the religious institution has multiple staff members, the religious leader seeks to provide a workplace that is healthy, supporting those things that keep staff in a joyful frame of service to others.
4. *Self-Awareness.* This aspect of servant leadership was covered in the description of an awakened heart. Suffice it to say, servant leaders know themselves well, their strengths and their weaknesses.
5. *Persuasion.* A good religious leader who is also a servant leader is not an authoritarian. The leader knows how to build consensus and be encouraging of those he or she serves.

6. *Conceptualization.* A servant leader is a dreamer. The everyday routine of just keeping the institution working can take a lot of time. A religious leader who is a servant leader will make time for visions and dreams. Retreats for spiritual renewal are absolutely necessary if such visioning and dreaming are to be part of the institutions we serve.

7. *Foresight.* This aspect of a servant leader has to do with studying the past experiences of one's leadership and of the religious institution he or she serves, identifying what is going on now and then making decisions based on what one has learned.

8. *Stewardship.* Whether we like it or not, congregations look up to religious leaders as the heads of the organizations they serve. In many systems, religious leaders have all the responsibility and very little authority. This, of course, is not fair, but it is a reality. Servant leaders take responsibility when it is theirs to take and lead by example.

9. *Commitment to the Growth of People.* A religious leader who is a good servant leader makes time for professional development . . . continuing education . . . and encourages those on his or her staff to continue to develop themselves professionally.

10. *Building Community.* This aspect of the servant leader has been thoroughly written about in other parts of this volume. Suffice it to say, building community is one of the most important aspects of a religious leader's ministry, not only for himself or herself but also for the community of faith he or she serves.[13]

A servant leader is a leader who leads out of one's heart. These religious leaders do not believe that they are perfect, and they certainly know the institutions that they serve are not perfect. A perfectionist personality does not fit very well into a leadership position within a congregation in today's world. And we would do well to be honest about our various flaws and imperfections if we want to relate to those who are spiritually hungry, persons who are looking not for perfection but for help and healing.

When I teach a class called The People Called Quakers, I share a warning to all those who are considering membership in Cincinnati Friends Meeting. In brief, I explain that communities of faith are not perfect institutions, and neither are the members who fill the pews on Sunday morning, who staff its committees, or who work to bring to life the beliefs that we hold in common. What does this mean? It means that if you are a part of this community of faith, one of two things will eventually happen. 1) You will disappoint the community, or 2) The community will disappoint you. The time may come when the community of faith doesn't do something that you believe is vitally important. We may fail to act on an issue or may even act in a manner contrary to what you expect. At the same time, it is possible that you might *not* do something that the community of faith asks of you or do it in a way that does not meet the expectations of other members. These disappointments are inevitable within a community of faith. Though such inevitable disappointments are sad, they are part of being *imperfect* people banding together in an *imperfect* way to create an *imperfect* institution. No amount of power or control exercised by the religious leader can change this imperfection. A heart-centered servant leader, however, who is aware of the drama going on within himself or herself and who understands his or her own imperfections is well suited to the needs of today's community of faith. Leading from the heart is a leadership model that understands where true power resides, a power that is centered in the Living God.

I began this chapter by quoting Thomas Kelly. It seems fitting to close it with another one of his insightful quotations, in which Kelly describes "life from the Center." The authors have used this quotation at the close of every *Sacred Chaos* seminar. It is in this Center where heart-centered religious leaders find their strength, because, as Kelly points out, if they are leading from an awakened heart that is centered in the love of God, they are not in control . . . God is:

> *Life from the Center is a life of unhurried peace and power. It is simple. It is serene. It is amazing. It is triumphant. It is radiant. It takes no time, but it occupies all our time. And it makes our life programs new and overcoming. We need not get frantic. God is at the helm. And when our little day is done, we lie down quietly in peace, for all is well.*[14]

Notes

1. Kelly, Thomas R. *A Testament of Devotion*. New York: Harper and Brothers, 1941.

2. Shores, Larry. "Richard P. Newby." *Star*, December 15, 1985.

3. Newby, James R. and Elizabeth S. Newby. *Between Peril and Promise*. Nashville: Thomas Nelson Publishers, 1984.

4. Woolman, John. *The Journal and Major Essays of John Woolman*. Edited by Amelia Gummere. New York: Macmillan, 1992.

5. Quindlen, Anna. "Life of the Closed Mind." *Newsweek*, May 29, 2005.

6. Will, George F. "The Oddness of Everything." *Newsweek*, May 22, 2005.

7. Frost, Robert. "Mending Wall." *North of Boston*. London: David Nutt, 1914.

8. Borg, Marcus J. *The Heart of Christianity: Rediscovering a Life of Faith*. San Francisco: HarperCollins, 2003.

9. Newby, James R. *Gathering the Seekers: Spiritual Growth Through Small Group Ministry.* New York: The Alban Institute, 1995.

10. Keen, Sam. "What You Ask Is Who You Are." *Spirituality and Health*, May 1, 2000.

11. "7 Examples of Self-Awareness in Everyday Life." April 21, 2020, by Kara McD. https://myquestionlife.com/examples-of-self-awareness-in-everyday-life/.

12. Fuerst, Tom. "3 Ways the Church Can Respond to the Capitol Building Riot." *Ministry Matters*, January 13, 2021. https://www.ministrymatters.com/all/entry/10676/3-ways-the-church-can-respond-to-the-capitol-building-riot.

13. Spears, Larry C. "Character and Servant Leadership: Ten Characteristics of Effective, Caring Leaders." *Journal of Virtues and Leadership* 1, no. 1 (2010).

14. Thomas Kelly. *A Testament of Devotion.* New York: Harper and Brothers, 1941.

5

~

Knowing Who You Are

Are you honest with yourself and others about your gifts and ministry expectations?
What is your spiritual autobiography? What is your personal credo . . . what you
believe and why you believe it?

It was Socrates who said, "To know thyself is the beginning of wisdom."
For religious leaders, such wisdom means, among other things, being honest
with oneself and others about one's gifts in ministry. Ministers, as much as
those they lead would like for them to be all things to all people, *are not* and
cannot be. At the beginning of any relationship between a community of faith
and a religious leader, this needs to be stated clearly. Hopefully, by the time
a religious leader becomes a religious leader, he or she has taken advantage
of some of the numerous gift- and personality-identification inventories that
will help them on the path of self-discovery. Only by understanding who
we are, by reflecting on the story that makes us who we are, can we lead
effectively.

Frederick Buechner delivered a series of lectures at Harvard University in
which he made the observation that all theology is at its heart *autobiography*,
and that what a theologian is doing essentially is examining as honestly as
he or she can the ups and downs of his or her own experience. Unless we
understand our lives as autobiographies that are continuously unfolding, we
are likely to take refuge in other people's stories and theology. This will lead
to ready-made ideologies and unexamined systems of belief as well as a lack
of authenticity in one's leadership. In short, religious leaders will find their
own theologies—what they believe and why they believe it—in the exami-
nation of the *experiences* of their lives.

In our *Sacred Chaos* seminars, we help religious leaders try to understand their life pilgrimages as *sacred* pilgrimages, i.e., their autobiographical

journeys, and help them make sense of their lives and the sacred search that makes them meaningful. We are helped in this pilgrimage of search, once again, by Frederick Buechner: "We search for a self to be. We search for other selves to love. We search for work to do. And since even when to one degree or another we find these things, we find also that there is still something crucial missing which we have not found, we search for that 'unfound thing' too, even though we do not know its name or where it is to be found or even if it is to be found at all."[1]

The "unfound thing" that Buechner mentions in our search, this process of understanding our sacred pilgrimage, is something for which I yearn, and it is that something for which we are *all* yearning. To put it succinctly, in the search for that "unfound thing," we are all on a journey of *trying to sort it all out.*

In the introduction to my book *Reflections from the Inner Light*, I write about my friend John who had been diagnosed with an inoperable, malignant brain tumor. He came to see me just after he had been to the doctor and received this unsettling news. "I am just trying to sort it all out," he said. He looked tired and strained as he held his head in his hands and wept. He called his diagnosis a death sentence, and now he was thinking about life issues that before this tragic news he had thought about with only passing attention. "Why me?" "Why did God allow this to happen to me?" "How will my family survive?" "How do I live the rest of my shortened life?" "What is God really like?" These were all questions that were part of our conversation, and there would be many more questions in the days to come. "I am just trying to sort it all out. . . ."[2] Although John's sorting was now on a fast track because of his diagnosis, it is a process in which we are all involved, a process that takes a lifetime to work through. Each of us is at various places along this sorting continuum, and regardless of stage of life, education, or profession, we are all on it. And religious leaders who find themselves in chaos are most assuredly on it.

There are four questions that have been helpful in my own process of trying to sort it all out, and they have been helpful to our *Sacred Chaos* participants as well. They are questions that have been asked over the centuries of human life on this earth.

First, *"How can I come to know with some certainty the meaning of human existence?"* Or, *"How do I find out who I am?"* In this first question, we focus on the process of revelation, or, "How have I experienced life so that I am helped in trying to understand who I am?" In the words of George Fox, "You will say, Christ saith this, and the apostles say this; *but what canst thou say?*"[3] "What is your experience?"

The most important truth that we know about the universe is that at one point in history, persons have emerged. Persons differ radically from any other beings known to us. Before persons emerged, there was an abundance of matter, but that was all. In Pascal's *Pensées*, he writes, "A human is but a reed, the most feeble thing in nature, but a human is a thinking reed. The entire universe need not arm itself to crush humans. A vapor, a drop of water suffices to kill them. But if the universe were to crush them, humans would still be nobler than that which killed them, because they know that they die and the advantage which the universe has over them; the universe knows nothing of this."[4]

Because persons are thinking, feeling creatures, they are experiencing their environment all the time. And because they can experience, they are absorbing revelation that is all around them. I believe that with each experience of life, God is revealing himself to us.

This past winter, I was sitting in my living room watching the various birds dine at our hanging bird feeder on the patio. Suddenly, a beautiful red cardinal flew down and landed in the midst of the gray-and-brown background that surrounded the feeder. There it was, in all its beautiful red splendor, with the brown of winter encircling everything around it. Now, I could have looked at it as just a bird eating some seeds in the dead of winter . . . big deal. Or, I could have seen it as a reminder of the beautiful array of nature that God has created, and how that beautiful, brightly colored bird was a sign from God that even when life is at its most brown and gray, which seems to be most days in an Ohio Valley winter, even when life is at its dullest period of the year, there is color, there is life, there is God.

Again, Frederick Buechner helps us: "The question is not whether the things that happen to you are chance things or God things because, of course, they are both at once. There is no chance thing through which God cannot speak—even the walk from the house to the garage that you walked ten thousand times before, even the moments when you cannot believe there is a God who speaks at all anywhere. God speaks, I believe, and the words he speaks are incarnate in the flesh and blood of ourselves and of our own footsore and sacred journeys."[5]

We find out who we are by asking, "How is God working in this experience of life?" And it is followed with the question, "What spiritual lessons am I learning from this experience?" Finally, as religious leaders, we need to ask, "How does this affect the way I do ministry?"

A second question along our journeys of search is this: *"What is the nature of that ultimate reality that sets limits and possibilities on my human existence?"*

As religious leaders, our response to this question is God, whose nature, we believe, is *love*. Such a response for Christians, however, is inseparable from our third, most important, question in our searches, which is *"Where in human historical experience can one turn to get help in deciding what is the meaning of human existence and the nature of ultimate reality?"* For Christians, our response is Jesus Christ.

In learning about Jesus, his life and teachings, we can grasp hold of the concrete, the historical, and the understandable. Jesus lived at a known point in history, which can be located through the various imperial regimes of the Roman Empire. He was a person who lived and died, and as Christians, we believe (or most of us believe) he rose from the dead. In Jesus, we find a teacher who can help us understand the nature of that ultimate reality that we call God. We believe that in Jesus, God became human, and in that transformation, the love of God became understandable.

The last of the important questions of life that can help us understand who we are is this: *"In what historical community is the meaning and purpose of human existence understood and its fulfillment best nurtured?"* Or, *"What community offers the most help?"* Again, for Christians, our response for more than two thousand years has been the gathered fellowship . . . the beloved community . . . the church.

Christianity is a social, relational faith. Jesus said, "Where two or three are gathered in my name, there am I among them" (Matthew 18:20). Where is the real presence? The real presence is in the gathered community, the beloved fellowship of the church, where one loving heart encourages another, and where our joys are multiplied and our sorrows are divided.

In these questions—"Who am I?" "Am I alone?" "What person in history is most worth listening to?" and "What community offers me the most help in trying to sort it all out?"—we are helped in the understanding of who we are and in the understanding of our journey as a sacred one . . . a journey that involves our continuous search for that "unfound thing" and for who we are in relationship to God and one another. Or, "Maybe the journey isn't so much about becoming anything. Maybe it's about *unbecoming* everything that isn't *really you* so you can be who you were meant to be in the first place."[6]

Knowing who we are as religious leaders is enhanced by the writing of our spiritual autobiographies. Writing these necessitates the discipline of reflective thinking about our lives and our purpose, and it encourages sensitivity to the working of God in our earthly journeys. Two possible outlines for writing a spiritual autobiography are below, or the religious leader may develop his or her own.

Method One:

1. Quickly list the important markers of your life. This list should not be made with careful consideration and extensive reflection. Rather, it is a "this is what comes to mind when I reflect upon my life."
   a. Significant people in your life.
   b. Significant events in your life.
   c. Significant experiences in your life.

Note: An event is a one-time experience: the birth of a child, graduation from college or seminary, the day of your marriage, the day of your divorce, the death of a parent or sibling. An experience is a process: pregnancy, your first job, a serious illness from which you recovered.

2. On a second day, join together people, events, and experiences in a chronological sequence. Include only those persons, events, and experiences that seem significant to you now.

As you make these connections between people, events, and experiences, look for the following:
   a. Trends or patterns.
   b. Ways God is active in your life.
   c. Principles you use to evaluate whether you feel God is active in your life.

You may also include your reflections on these:
   d. An understanding of your relationship with Christ.
   e. Theological concepts that have been illumined by your life experiences.
   f. Commitments you have made because of your experiences.
   g. A sense of Christian vocation that has developed, i.e., your calling as a religious leader.
   h. Ways you have matured in your spiritual life or a pattern in your devotional life.
   i. Areas in life that represent successes and areas in life that remain ongoing concerns.

3. Take an intuitive leap into your future.
   a. What do you see as forward directions to be pursued?
   b. Are there goals to be achieved or commitments to be made?

Method Two:

1. Develop a lifeline in any manner you wish. You may use a line, spiral, diagram, or timeline. Focus on transitions, changes, decisions, new

directions, and marker events. It is often helpful to show geographical locations, schools, work settings, role statuses (child, single adult, married), significant figures and events, and pluses and minuses of each period. In a workshop, author and teacher Sam Keen had us make drawings of the houses in which we were raised, remembering the various rooms and activities that took place there. He emphasized that those rooms and activities that we *cannot* remember are the most important for us *to* remember.

2. Identify key transition periods. Evaluate each one as easy or difficult on a scale of one (easy) to ten (difficult). Think about the reason for each rating, e.g., "not ready to move on" or "a disturbing external event" or "experienced much inner suffering."

3. Reflect upon your timeline using the following questions:
   a. Where did I experience God's presence or absence?
   b. Over which transitions did I have the most or least control?
   c. Where were the high and low points?
   d. Where were the transitions smooth? traumatic?
   e. What issues were dominant during various periods?
   f. Were any issues left unresolved?
   g. Are there patterns or trends?

The writing of one's spiritual autobiography should be a joy and not a chore. It is a good way to begin the process of reflective thinking about one's life. The following is a simple example of what one might do in writing a spiritual autobiography. It is important to note, however, that there is no set formula for such a writing.

I was born in Minneapolis, Minnesota. My parents were Quakers, and my father was a Quaker minister. My family, as far as I can research, have been Quakers for as long as there has been a Quaker movement, extending back to the mid-1600s. The only slippage in this tradition was when my great-great-great-grandfather was disowned from his Meeting for marrying a Methodist!

I am a Christian and I am a Quaker because I was born into these traditions. And so the first stage of my faith development was tradition centered. It did not take me long to learn how unique this tradition is. Throughout my years of schooling in Minneapolis and later in Muncie, Indiana, I was the only Quaker in my class.

A few summers ago, while studying at Princeton Theological Seminary, I was perusing some of the new book releases in the campus bookstore. I saw a biography of James Dean, the actor, and knowing that he grew up in a Quaker home in Fairmount, Indiana, I quickly opened the book to learn what the author had said about the Quaker influence on Dean. The biographer opened the chapter on the subject with these words: "A Quaker is one who can take the pomp out of any circumstance!" As one who loves parties and fun get-togethers, I found this hurtful and disappointing!

As I reflect on my grade-school and high-school years, I realize I made every effort to put the pomp back into every circumstance. I was rebellious by nature and enjoyed all the trappings of a popular social life. I was attending parties every Friday and Saturday night, and my 1956 Chevy became for me a spiritual icon.

After graduation from high school in Muncie, I moved with my parents to Wichita, Kansas, where my father became the minister at University Friends Meeting. I became a student at Friends University. These were the years that were filled with tumult . . . Vietnam, civil rights, campus unrest, and general social upheaval. During my four years in college, I moved from being merely tradition-centered in my faith to being activist-centered. My Christian Quaker faith took on new meaning as I began to understand the radical dimensions of Jesus's teachings, and the Quaker concerns for simplicity, peace, integrity, community, equality, and stewardship of the earth provided a springboard for my own social-activist concerns. I majored in sociology and prepared to become a social worker in the inner city, where I would clean up all of society's problems within a few weeks. Youthful idealism fueled my compassion and impatience for injustice. I couldn't graduate quickly enough!

I was married during my junior year in college, and I accepted a position working the three-to-eleven shift as a respiratory therapy technician in a local hospital. I found myself listening to my father's sermons more carefully, and even began considering the possibility of becoming a minister. Six months prior to graduation, Central City Friends Meeting in Nebraska invited me to become their minister. I accepted this call, and almost immediately learned that I would become a father.

Alicia Marie was born and became the newest member of Central City Friends Meeting. As I continued in my pastoral work in Nebraska, I was feeling inadequate. The more I read in the area of Christian and Quaker thought, the more I realized the need for more education. After just two years in Central City, we moved to Ohio, where I could be close to the Earlham School of Religion. It was here where I began my studies for the master of divinity degree. As I moved in my faith development from tradition-centered to activist-centered, I was now moving from activist-centered to intellect-centered. I became captivated by the pursuit of knowledge and the development of my intellect. I would go to class at Earlham in the morning, and in the afternoon I would go over to Elton Trueblood's study, Teague Library, and study with him.

In four years, I graduated from the Earlham School of Religion and soon thereafter accepted a position in Richmond, Indiana, as the director of the Yokefellow Institute and assistant to Elton Trueblood. I later joined the faculty of the Earlham School of Religion, where I served as the director of the D. Elton Trueblood

Academy. While on the faculty, I went through a time of chaos in my life . . . my father died, Elton Trueblood died, my mother died, our only child graduated from high school and went to Michigan for college, and my wife, Elizabeth, and I went through a divorce. Through all this chaos, a new dimension to my life began to emerge. This new direction found expression in some words from an essay I wrote on faith and knowledge:

"In the cosmic theatre of life, I have been pondering just how important all of this attention to academic excellence is. It is a question I raise each time I hear of a student suicide or learn about a student selling his or her ethics down the river in order to secure a good grade. There is a lot of pressure in a good academic institution. The torch of knowledge is the center of worship.

"And yet what is knowledge without the wonder of faith? Learned information is of little use to the world if it is not coupled with the formation of the spirit. A good liberal arts college will try hard to keep spiritual discovery and academic discovery in balance. But deep down I believe that if push comes to shove, a good denominational-centered college will sacrifice their concern for spirituality on the altar of academic achievement.

"The idolatry of reason is a big problem at good colleges and is a bigger problem for the professors who live and die in the world of academia. I find that the wonder of faith can temper this academic disease, and I am always impressed by learned persons who not only have a 'clear-head of reason' with a 'tender-heart of faith.' It is a difficult combination to keep in balance, but it is this combination, I believe, that will lead to human wholeness."

I left Earlham for Plymouth Congregational Church in Des Moines, Iowa, and during this time, my book Sacred Chaos was released. Elizabeth and I eventually remarried, and after a time at the Wayzata Community Church in Wayzata, Minnesota, and the Church of the Savior in Oklahoma City, Oklahoma, we are now in Cincinnati, back home in our Quaker tradition.

My faith journey has taken me through several stages, from tradition-centered to activist-centered to intellect-centered to heart-centered. Regardless of the particular focus, I have found that all these elements are important if we are to grow spiritually. When we have a healthy understanding of our tradition and know the importance of keeping that tradition alive by being active in peace and social-justice concerns, and we are able to defend our faith intellectually as well as be sensitive to the concerns of the heart, we have at least begun the process of living in a spiritually wholistic way.

If we are to fully understand who we are as religious leaders, then along with the writing of our spiritual autobiographies, we need to ask ourselves, "What do I believe and why do I believe it?" As I have reflected on my own life experience and search, certain foci have become clear, which I share here as an example of such a reflective theological task.

First, I believe in the words of Alfred North Whitehead, that God is "a richly related being whose innermost nature is in his ceaseless participation and sharing."[7] This is a God of process, a God who is on a journey with me. Although Whitehead is our best-known process thinker, the understanding of process theology can be traced to Heraclitus, who said, "You cannot step twice into the same river; for fresh waters are ever flowing in upon you." The foundational premise of process or journey theology is the belief that everything is in a state of flux, and everything is in the process toward becoming something. From Heraclitus to John Travolta, who said in the movie Phenomenon, "Everything is on its way somewhere," journey theology has convinced me that we are all on a journey, and I believe that in each moment of this journey, God is interacting with us.

Second, relationship is a very important part of my theology. I see God in my relationships with others. I believe that there is that of God in every person, and as I interact with others, whether it is encouraging the discouraged, feeding the hungry, or sitting with a friend over coffee or beer, my understanding of God is broadened and deepened, thus making me a relational theologian.

And my understanding of relational theology extends beyond the human world to the world of nature. As I write these words, it is a very cold and dark day in Indian Hill, Ohio. A few flakes of snow are falling and there is a slight breeze. In the distance are two deer foraging for food and periodically looking up at a passing car along Keller Road. Trying not to lament the winter we are in, remembering fall and looking forward to spring, I seek, instead, to experience the here and now, recognizing my oneness with this hour and with this day in which I am now living. As a relational theologian, I know that my interactions in the natural world are important to my understanding of how God interacts with me. In the miracle of the natural world and the season of winter, I can feel the presence of God speaking to me.

Third, my experience has led me to understand that God is a God of justice. Throughout the Hebrew and Christian Testaments, justice is a recurring theme. From my earliest times in life, I can remember the pursuit of justice to be a part of who my family was and who I have become. We were a family who took the Quaker testimony of equality seriously. There has been the lifelong pursuit of justice for African Americans that my father and mother instilled within me. Through my mother's work with Church Women United and my father's work as the chair of the mayor's commission on human relations in Minneapolis, Muncie, and Wichita, I was introduced to the struggle for racial equality in America. In my work with Elizabeth, a Hispanic woman who grew up in a migrant farm-laborer family (see her book, A Migrant with Hope: A Memoir of Peril and Promise), I have been involved with justice issues surrounding this country's treatment of migrant farmworkers and the way immigrants have been treated at our southern border. I know that our history in this country, what is considered a predominantly

Christian country, is not one of equal justice for all. The way in which the belief in Manifest Destiny led to the wholesale killings of Native Americans, and the lasting effects of slavery, the original sin of America, continue to haunt us. There was the turning away from our shores of the ship St. Louis carrying Jewish refugees from Nazi Germany, as well as the Chinese Exclusion Act, which have stained the words we find on the Statue of Liberty: "Give me your tired, your poor, / Your huddled masses yearning to breathe free." And now brown people at our southern border who are seeking asylum and a better life are being treated unjustly. The God of justice and love who I worship and who is a central part of my belief system weeps at these kinds of actions.

A God of journey, a God of relationship, and a God of justice are central to my theology. At the center of these core pieces of what I believe, however, is the belief that God is love. As my sacred journey continues, filled with perils from both within and without as well as experiences of joy and love from both within and without, I will continue to write my theology, as we are all doing, whether consciously or unconsciously. As my understanding of God continues to unfold, I will continue to seek the God of journey, relationship, justice, and love in all my life experiences. And I believe this God of love will continue to seek me.

Perhaps the best tool that we have for understanding who we are is the keeping of a journal. At the beginning of each *Sacred Chaos* seminar, participants are given a journal for use throughout the week together. It is hoped that the discipline of journal-writing that they learn during the week of *Sacred Chaos* will become a part of their spiritual discipline when they return home.

How much time should we spend on this creative task? The amount of time spent, as well as the length of writing, will vary. Ten minutes spent writing one or two pages about a frustrating work situation may well be sufficient to discover how God is present. Reflection on a passage of Scripture or other reading may take several days of writing for longer periods. In essence, each time we work on a sermon, we are journaling. In writing a sermon, we are interacting with a passage of Scripture, sharing our experiences as illustrations and working out our own theology as we write and speak.

One of the most important elements in journaling is setting aside a regular time to do it. This time becomes honored each day as an important appointment. One should attempt to write in his or her journal several times each week. A daily routine, many have discovered, works best. It also is important to find the right place. Quiet surroundings provide the right atmosphere for writing, as well as a comfortable chair and good lighting. It helps the creative process if the same location is used each day.

Journaling in this context is supposed to help religious leaders in their search to understand themselves, as well as to understand what they believe and why they believe it. The following questions may be helpful as a way to begin the journaling process:

Who is God to you? Who is Jesus? Who is the Christ? Who are you? Do you believe that humans are fallen? sinful? ignorant? Why? How? What is sin? How have you experienced God? Jesus? the Holy Spirit? How important is the Bible to your life of faith? your work and ministry? What are your favorite passages of Scripture? What are your favorite books of the Bible? Why? What is grace? What is forgiveness? What does salvation mean to you? When have you experienced grace or forgiveness? When have you forgiven another? How does God fit into your experience of human forgiveness? What does transformation look like? How does it occur? Can you see patterns of dying to old ways and coming alive again in your experience? What have been your awakening or transformative moments? Who has been instrumental in these experiences?

Finally . . . *What was your day like today? With whom did you relate well? poorly? How could you see God moving in your relationships today? What happened today . . . this week . . . that relates to your theological perceptions (God, Jesus, sin, grace, faith)? How have you grown in your faith from when you first began your ministry?*

These questions can help religious leaders become unstuck about journal writing. The key to your journaling is to be *comfortable*. It is not about being neat; it is about being honest with yourself, which may necessitate erasing, adding, rethinking an issue or problem, or ripping out pages that no longer are helpful. Note: Your journal is *your journal*. It is where you write about your most intimate thoughts and concerns. Keep it in a safe place to which only you have access.

Another helpful tool in our self-discovery search and understanding of who we are is the use of what Quakers call "clearness committees." These committees are formed when an individual asks for help with a problem, or when a couple is planning on getting married, or when a change in vocation is in the offing, or any number of other times when we need help from the community of faith in discerning our lives' directions. Britain Yearly Meeting describes how a *meeting for clearness* should be designed:

> Meetings for clearness should be held in a relaxed atmosphere of trust. . . . A facilitator should be chosen to assist in clarifying the question or questions being asked. Some groups may decide that notes should be taken. It will have to be made explicit that confidentiality is to be maintained within the group. There is need for listening with undivided attention, for tact, affirmation, and love for those seeking clearness.
>
> Each member of the group should have opportunities to question and explore the background to the matter that is to be clarified. It is important

not to be diverted by side-issues but to concentrate on exploring options and understanding underlying difficulties. It will take time to reach clearness and periods of gathered worship will be helpful.

A further meeting or meetings may be needed if the original issue, or practical details, would benefit from further thought. When clearness is reached, the group should be laid down.[8]

In fact, in many ways our *Sacred Chaos* seminars resemble clearness committees. Some attendees have participated because they are struggling with the issue of whether to continue in the ministry. Others need guidance about whether to change ministry locations or retire. Still others have serious questions about their ministerial effectiveness and need help with some new ideas that will help them change their old patterns and begin a new path. The point is that we need one another to help in the major decisions of our lives, and we are helped when we receive advice, care, and encouragement from our faith communities.

If we are in the throes of chaos, to *remember* becomes a most significant spiritual exercise along our journeys of self-discovery. In his book *To a Dancing God*, Sam Keen writes about an encounter with a man while Sam was constructing a redwood fence around his home. The man, who was walking his dog, stopped and watched Sam for a while, and then inquired if he could help. Sam told him he could, but before the conversation could go further, the man explained that he had been injured by a small piece of metal that had torn into his brain, lodging in the area that stores and controls memory. The man survived the accident, but it had left him with no control over his memory. There were times he could remember events that had just occurred, and there were other times he could remember events from long ago. But he was unable to keep the two in balance. This lack of a dependable memory kept the man from employment and planning for the future. Because of this, he asked Sam to write his name and address on a piece of paper, which he could use to remind himself of the encounter. Sam relates what happened next: "We planned to meet on the following Monday and work on the fence together, but he never appeared. I imagine that he found the slip of paper on which I had written my name and address in his pocket and could not recall how it got there."[9]

What are we without our memories? Each of us is shaped and molded by experiences that are unique to the individual. Without memories of those experiences, how do we define who we are? Our past weaves our present. Who we are today, and the experiences we encounter, will create tomorrow's possibilities. How tragic for the man whose memory was disturbed, for he is destined to never connect with anyone or anything—confined to a limbo of passing moments, without a history and, consequently, without a future.

A few years ago, I began the process of mining my own personal mythology, reflecting and remembering. As a way to begin such an exercise, I went back to the old neighborhood I had known as a boy and slowly walked the streets. There are special places in everyone's lives where they would like time to stand still. One such place is the neighborhood in which one grew up. For many who are in difficult home situations, "the neighborhood" can be a source of stability. Each day brings many changes, but the old neighborhood is known territory. When I was growing up, I knew every alley, every yard, every tree, and every fence within a two-mile radius from my front door. I knew which opening in which fence I could pass my bike through, and which yards to avoid because of hostile dogs or adults. There was a sense of security in knowing all of this. I knew that there was always one area of Muncie, Indiana, where my knowledge of the territory provided a safe place.

I believe that all of life is sacramental. Whether this sacrament of God in one's life is experienced along the streets and alleys of one's old neighborhood or in a time of worship at Westminster Abbey, it is the *reality* of the spiritual experience, not the form of the sacrament, that is important.

Being in touch with the memories of the neighborhood in which we grew up and all those nodal or awakening moments when we learned the important spiritual truths about ourselves, as well as remembering those important relationships in our lives that have made us who we are, evokes within us the truth that knowing *who we are* also will help us understand *whose we are*.

Self-discovery is also God-discovery. And the search for God and an understanding of who we are is forever unfolding. It is a lifelong process.

Notes

1. Buechner, Frederick. *The Sacred Journey: A Memoir of Early Days.* New York: HarperCollins, 1982.

2. Newby, James R. *Reflections from the Inner Light: A Journal of Quaker Spirituality.* Eugene: Wipf and Stock Publishers, 2019.

3. Fox, George. *The Journal of George Fox.* Edited by John Nickalls. Philadelphia: Philadelphia Yearly Meeting, 1997.

4. Pascal, Blaise. *Pensées.* New York: Penguin Classics, 1995.

5. Buechner, Frederick. *The Sacred Journey: A Memoir of Early Days.* New York: HarperCollins, 1982..

6. <www.contemplativemonk.com>.

7. Pittenger, Norman. *Alfred North Whithead.* Cambridge: Lutterworth Press, 1967.

8. Britain Yearly Meeting. *Quaker Faith and Practice.* Warwick: Warwick Printing Company, 1995.

9. Keen, Sam. *To a Dancing God.* New York: Harper and Row, 1970.

PART II

~

JOURNEY OUTWARD

6

~

A New Institutional Landscape

How has the pandemic changed the ways you do ministry? What are the issues centered around justice for the poor and racial equality, and how are you and your faith community addressing them? How are you addressing the issues associated with the "nones" and "dones"?

A friend of mine refers to our time as a time of existential trauma. We are not only facing the prospect of a pandemic that never ends, but we also are in a period of great social upheaval and deep social rifts. It is one of those transition periods in history, when everything is open to question, even the most basic spiritual pillars undergirding Western civilization. NPR's Krista Tippett has written, "We are in a communal collective, global transition . . . moving from one reality to another that we can't see. Part of the work, the calling now is to stand really respectfully before how very unsettling and stress-filled this is." It is indeed a time of chaos.

In recent months, we watched in horror as thousands fled Afghanistan following the takeover by the Taliban. America, once again, in what seems like a broken record, is turning inward trying to understand why our foreign policy, and this time a twenty-year commitment to a country that cost us $220 million per day, has ended so badly. We have a political system that is in a constant state of gridlock. Racism continues to haunt us and is played out in an unjust economic system designed to maintain the status quo, i.e., white power and control. Our infrastructure has been neglected for years, and it will take decades for us to repair it. We have an immigration system that is completely broken. With each mass shooting, we become more and more numb to gun violence. And there is a collapse of meaning and declining influence of some of society's basic institutions, including religious institutions. The "nones" and the "dones" are the fastest-growing group of persons when polled about their religious affiliation. In the words of Lewis Brogdon, "Daily we witness the spectacles of rampant cynicism, violence, discord, neglect of the vulnerable members of society, profound moral confusion and a kind of irrationality that is utterly baffling, like those who believe the pandemic was some hoax or those latching on to conspiracy theories."[1] How are religious leaders coping in such a culture? And, in this time of horror and grief, how do we as religious leaders help those in our communities of faith learn to cope?

As difficult as it is for some to see right now, I believe that religious leaders and the communities of faith they serve can play a major role in responding to the various crises before us. Like the lava flowing across the earth from an erupting volcano, there is a new landscape forming. Religious institutions are being forced to respond to the new realities with which we are confronted. Even though it is hard to reflect upon what we are experiencing at the moment and find anything more than horror and grief, some observations can be made. How we cope now and address the spiritual issues that are emerging from the changing spiritual landscape will do much to help us envision new futures for our ministries. First, the pandemic.

When I was in seminary, one of my professors said, "If you want to understand what natural evil looks like, read *The Plague* by Albert Camus." In recent months, as we have been going through our own plague of the twenty-first century, I have been rereading Camus in an effort to grasp at some kind of response from history for what we are dealing with now. In describing All Souls' Day in the midst of the plague year, Camus writes,

> In the plague year people no longer wished to be reminded of their dead. Because, indeed, they were thinking all too much about them as it was. There was no more question of revisiting them with a shade of regret and much melancholy. They were no longer the forsaken to whom, one day in the year, you came to justify yourself. They were intruders whom you would rather forget. This is why the Day of the Dead this year was tacitly but willfully ignored. As Cottard dryly remarked—Tarrou noted that the habit of irony was growing on him more and more—*each day was for us a Day of the Dead*. (italics mine)

And in the last paragraph of *The Plague*, the character Rieux is listening to the cries of joy rising from the town as they celebrate the end of the plague, and warns us that such joy is always imperiled: "He knew what those jubilant crowds did not know but could have learned in books: that the plague bacillus never dies or disappears for good; that it can lie dormant for years and years in furniture and linen-chests; that it bides its time in bedrooms, cellars, trunks, and bookshelves; and that perhaps the day would come when, for the bane and the enlightening of men, it would rouse up its rats again and send them forth to die in a happy city."[2] As humans should have learned through the centuries, we are a very vulnerable species.

By the time this book is published, it is hoped that we will have come out on the other side of what has been a multiyear nightmare. With each new variant, the pandemic raises its ugly head once again and strikes at the most vulnerable . . . the unvaccinated, children, the elderly, and those with chronic diseases, like diabetes. The cycle that this pandemic has put our institutions through—restaurants, the travel industry, as well as our communities of faith—has caused serious damage. Where I worship, we went into a time of only Zoom worship for almost a year, then we opened up and went without masks if one had been vaccinated. From here, and following the CDC guidelines, we went back to wearing masks, even if fully vaccinated, and encouraged social distancing. Because of the fast-spreading Omicron variant, we went back to only Zoom worship. This kind of a crazy cycle is causing considerable anxiety among congregants and their religious leaders. And, quite frankly, people are just plain tired of having to deal with the rapid changes in lifestyle that the pandemic is forcing upon us.

Several pastors I know are struggling to discover a new normal in the wake of the pandemic. The statistics are not fully in or currently reliable. As we all know, many congregations have turned to virtual worship services, fellowship opportunities, and business responsibilities during the pandemic. Many religious leaders believe now that a virtual alternative to in-person worship and fellowship will be with us into the future. As with the corporate and business world, many employees are finding that their productivity is just as high working remotely as when they went to work in person. When one considers the overhead of a building, the time involved, and the cost of operating a vehicle, it is not surprising that the crisis of the pandemic brought about new possibilities and financial benefits to the world of work. Now the religious communities are facing a set of dilemmas. It appears that there is a "virtual church" and an "in-person church" within the same congregation; and more and more, it appears likely that some form of this dichotomy will continue after the pandemic. Providing taped productions for those who are unable to attend the worship services, many churches met the needs of their membership in long-term care facilities or with restricted ambulatory and mobile needs. This virtual approach now allows for many, at least those who have sufficient internet access, to continue their participation in the life of their congregation. Many people have become involved in worship and study opportunities from a distance and are enjoying some meaningful experiences of spiritual connection, growth, and ministry. If two churches exist within the same congregation, how will the groups integrate into the whole experience of community? Perhaps smaller congregations will have their own versions of what megachurches learned long ago about how to connect in a church within a church. Many religious leaders are ready for such a new normal. Many others are not. The bottom line is that religious leaders are in the thick of an ongoing stressful season in ministry, with many, like Ron, wondering whether it is sustainable for them.

Ron felt called into the ministry over thirty years ago, and, in many ways, he has felt blessed to preach hope, provide compassionate pastoral care, and lead congregations into ministries in their local communities. However, nothing quite prepared him for the variety of challenges that he would face during the lengthy limitations and restrictions required through the months, turned years, of the COVID-19 pandemic. His own emotional needs from necessary social support and caring friendships were not being met. He was uncertain about how to nurture his own spiritual growth, in terms of both the loss of such fellowship and the high anxiety that was disruptive of his spirit. Again and again, he found himself in avoidant behaviors of reading one mystery after the other, watching meaningless television, and playing video games. The pressure to make the church experience successful seemed well beyond his own capabilities. He found it difficult to find individuals in the congregation who could assist with all the complexities of livestreaming. The congregation was losing a sense of connection, that spiritual and emotional togetherness that they had when they met in person. Ron simply could not see a way forward, and, as he was only experiencing more and more of a sense of failure and guilt, he decided to resign without another commitment to provide pastoral ministry to another congregation. Finding other work temporarily while contemplating early retirement, he was now in the midst of pondering his future relationship with the church, any church, and the more it seemed that the virtual church would now be a part of the new normal, he did not see a return to serving the institutional church. To find a sense of comfort with his awareness of a call to serve God and God's people, Ron was looking for small opportunities to do ministry—a one-on-one conversation here, words of encouragement there, or volunteering in a homeless shelter.

In a message on Facebook, Anne Lamott, the author of such best sellers as *Traveling Mercies*, expresses Ron's frustrations, and all our frustrations with what the pandemic has done to our lives:

> This year I have our collective condition on my heart, which is existential exhaustion, disbelief and disorientation. I keep thinking bitterly that I am just *done*, like an overcooked rump roast; just *done*. I have been an excellent sport for nearly two years—think Dinah Shore with dreadlocks. Grace, which always bats last, saw me through pretty much unscathed relative to most people in the world, although a few scathes have come up recently. But the good

sportsmanship was based on this all coming to an end at some point, and right now I am not convinced that it will. It's like being in a whiteout where you can't easily tell which is up and which is down or sideways.[3]

As a result of this whiteout, many religious leaders are calling it quits. In his book *God and the Pandemic*, theologian N. T. Wright offers a response to our grim circumstances:

> In a time of acute crisis, when death sneaks into houses and shops, when you may feel healthy yourself but you may be carrying the virus without knowing it, when every stranger on the street is a threat, when we go around in masks, when churches are shut and people are dying with nobody to pray by their bed-side—this is a time for lament. For admitting we don't have easy answers. For refusing to use the crisis as a loudspeaker for what we'd been wanting to say in any case. For weeping at the tomb of our friends. For the inarticulate groaning of the Spirit. 'Rejoice with those who rejoice,' said Paul, 'and weep with those who weep.' Yes, and the world is weeping right now. The initial calling of the Church, first and foremost, is to take our place humbly among the mourners.[4]

Whenever we go through a time of rapid change and shock to our systems of belief, we take refuge in those familiar institutions where we can *mourn* and that give us *hope*. We seek a more intense connection with what we know . . . our families . . . our churches, synagogues, and mosques. During the most horrific times of life, the faith community . . . the beloved community . . . has been the traditional institution to which we have always turned for sharing grief and offering comfort and hope.

The 9/11 attack occurred during my tenure as the minister of spiritual growth at Plymouth Congregational Church in Des Moines, Iowa. It was a Tuesday morning, and I was in the midst of leading a breakfast meeting, what we called AMENS—All Men Experiencing Nurturing Spirituality—when I first heard the news of the attack on the Twin Towers. Immediately I called home and checked in with my wife. Just hearing her voice provided comfort. Then, the Plymouth staff, who were getting ready for their weekly meeting together, threw out the regular agenda and began planning for a time of wor-ship that evening. It was a day of chaos, with persons coming to the church to sit in the sanctuary and pray . . . to talk with one of the ministers . . . to weep with other congregants, and to try to make sense out of what was *nonsense*. That evening, as we gathered in that place of spiritual comfort and hope, the sanctuary was full to overflowing.

Religious institutions and religious leaders are in the business of providing a spiritual anchor during these times of cultural turmoil. People are searching for *stability* and *hope*. They want assurance that, in the end, all shall be well. Religious institutions and religious leaders are in that important position to be able to offer people this hope and stability, as well as to help people mourn.

A second thing that occurs during times of great stress is that people develop a more intense concern for meaning . . . meaning in their work . . . meaning in their family lives . . . meaning that gives their lives a sense of purpose and passion. What is really important in this life? I believe that people are resigning from their jobs in record numbers during this pandemic because they have asked this question and felt that what they were doing did not match up with what is really important.

Tragedy and suffering always take us back to the basics. What we are experiencing today helps us realize that, ultimately, life is not about acquiring as much as we can in our four-score years on this earth, nor is it about finding new and creative ways to gobble up the earth's resources. No, tragedy and loss, pain and suffering move us to the *spiritual basics*, which were summarized by Jesus in response to the question asked by the lawyer. What are the spiritual basics? *To love God and to love one another.* This is what really matters, and the expressions of these basics can be found in the countless acts of love and caring that are taking place throughout the world as people struggle to understand the new normal of their lives.

I recently attended a writers' workshop at Princeton Theological Seminary. The aforementioned Anne Lamott was one of the presenters. In the question-and-answer period following one of her presentations, she was asked, "How do we respond to the current political and social environment in our country?" In essence, her response was, "Go out and feed the hungry, care for the sick, love the unlovable, and give people hope that our better angels will win out in the end." As overwhelming as our problems are, and however numbed we are by the needs facing us, we can all do what Lamott suggests. That old song says we should brighten the corner where we live, and that is something we can all do, and it is in the brightening of our corners that we can find meaning.

As I have counseled with persons throughout this pandemic and during this time of social rifts and widening divisions, I have encouraged people to express their righteous indignation over what has befallen us. Anger is an appropriate response to what we are going through. I have felt it, and you have felt it, and it is all right to feel it! We seek justice. We seek to understand, for example, who is responsible for the January 6 insurrection. We seek to understand how and why the pandemic has been so destructive, with over one million Americans already dead from this virus. I do not understand how one of the wealthiest nations in the world could be so unprepared for a virus pandemic. One of the statistics I heard was that the United States has approximately 4 percent of the world's population, and yet we have 25 percent of the COVID-19 cases.[5] One of the saddest articles I read about this virus was how the group Doctors Without Borders has come to America to help the Navajo Nation, which has been especially hard-hit by the pandemic. Think about this . . . Doctors Without Borders coming to our country to do their missionary work! This is a group that is known for its work in third-world nations. Is our country so ill prepared and in such dire straits that we have to rely on a group such as this to bring qualified medical help to our own people?[6]

I believe that we are still a people of justice, that we need to study and learn how we have arrived at where we are and find out how we can repair our social safety net so that we can be ready for future experiences of similar pandemics, as well as seek ways to heal our divisions.

I know that many would like to blame Donald Trump for what has befallen us. The truth is our country was on a trajectory of divisiveness long before Trump entered the political arena. What he did was *exploit* the divisions that many see as an economy that was working for only the wealthy, and he exploited the ugly undercurrent of racism that surfaced after eight years of an African American president and has worsened as America has become browner and blacker. When we begin to look critically at the history of our country, we will see a troubling picture of entrenched racism. And as religious leaders, when we look critically at the institutions we serve, we will discover that there is much more that we can be doing to correct this troubling picture of racial injustice.

I was a small boy when I first learned about racism. Although I went to a school that did not have any African American students, my father taught me about racial injustice through his work as the chair of the human-relations council in both Minneapolis, Minnesota, and Muncie, Indiana. One example of my father confronting racism stands out in my memory. I was eight or nine years old when I was sitting in the car with my father as we traveled on Madison Avenue in Muncie. All of a sudden, my father pulled the car to the curb and told me to stay seated. He climbed out of the car and walked up to an unfamiliar house. Flying from the porch was a Confederate flag. I watched as my father knocked on the door of the house, and a man came to greet him. There was some conversation that I could not hear, and soon my father returned to the car. I watched the man with whom my father had been conversing slowly take down the Confederate flag, wrap it in his arms, and take it inside the house. As we left, continuing our journey down Madison Avenue,

I asked my father what he had said to the man. He said, "I told him that the flag he was flying was offensive to a large number of residents of Muncie, because it represented the glorification of slavery. I told him that he had every right to fly the flag, but it would help race relations in our community if he would take it down." I know it is hard to believe that this incident did not end with my father getting a fist in his face, but it ended peacefully, with the man doing the right thing by taking the flag down.

Such early experiences of action against racism have led me to become an active member of the advisory board of a racial justice initiative called A Mighty Stream. This is a new effort in the city of Cincinnati to help faith leaders examine issues surrounding racial injustice and how these faith leaders can respond to such injustice. The effort is spearheaded by an interfaith organization called EquaSion, with its executive director, Chip Harrod, providing leadership. In the newly published "Discussion Guide on Race and Racial Equity" released by A Mighty Stream, it says this "program aims to organize and unite Cincinnati's diverse communities of faith into a moral force to act in ways that will remediate race-based systemic inequities wherever they occur. . . . We believe that a central, ongoing part of anti-racism work is the time and vulnerability to reflect on our individual and communal biases, shortcomings and history."[7] A Mighty Stream is asking faith communities to adopt the following resolutions:

1. We resolve to discern our personal and communal biases and commit to transforming our lives for the greater good;
2. We resolve to listen to and learn from one another as we pursue anti-racism and racial justice in our personal and corporate lives;
3. We resolve to address racism and racial disparities and systemic inequities in our spheres of influence; and
4. We resolve as an interfaith community to work with civic leaders and elected officials in advocating for policies that dismantle structural racism and the ideology of white supremacy.

This program is new, and it is bringing together the myriad expressions of faith found in the community of Cincinnati to help our city work through its problems with racism. It is a program that has been inaugurated because of the murder of George Floyd in Minneapolis, but it is dealing with an issue that has been with us since the founding of America.

Robert P. Jones claims that our time is a time of reckoning. He says, "The tumultuous events of 2020 have called the question about where we white Christians stand on white supremacy. History is recording a roll call vote that requires us to declare our position." He goes on to write about how we can remain supportive of our white heritage and become defensive through inaction. "Or we can rededicate ourselves to the work of handing down a healthier faith and country to our children and our children's children." He emphasizes that we cannot do both and pleads for us to choose a future in which we stand with our Black and brown brothers and sisters "to achieve the promise of a multiracial and multi-religious America."[8]

In her wonderful and insightful book *Caste: The Origins of Our Discontents*, Isabel Wilkerson writes,

> With our current ruptures, it is not enough to not be racist or sexist. Our times call for being pro-African American, pro-woman, pro-Latino, pro-Asian, pro-Indigenous, pro-humanity in all its manifestations. In our era, it is not enough to be tolerant. You tolerate mosquitoes in the summer, a rattle in an engine, the gray slush that collects at the crosswalk in winter. You tolerate what you would rather not have to deal with and wish would go away. It is no honor to be tolerated. Every spiritual tradition says love your neighbor, not yourself, not tolerate them. . . . None of us choose the circumstances of our birth. We had nothing to do with having been born into privilege or under stigma. We have everything to do with what we do with our God-given talents and how we treat others in our species from this day forward.[9]

On page after page of the Christian Testament, Jesus challenges us to imagine a life together in which the poor are blessed, the hungry are fed, and the stranger is welcomed. And what we may find in accepting this challenge is new life for us and for our congregations. Today's religious leaders and the congregations they serve do not have the privilege of doing *nothing* in the face of the challenges that Jesus sets forth. Our call is *not* to be comfortable in a culture that is filled with the discomforts that many are suffering. We are being called to become vulnerable by doing what Isabel Wilkerson challenges us to do . . . to become pro–African American by working in such programs as A Mighty Stream; to become pro-woman by supporting the vulnerable women and children who find comfort and support in safe houses in our communities; to become pro-Latino, and in doing so, becoming pro-immigrant by becoming solidarity congregations with the Sanctuary Movement, which is fighting an unjust immigration system; to become pro-LGBTQ by becoming congregations that are open and affirming. By accepting the challenge of Jesus to make our communities of faith into all-inclusive, diverse, beloved communities free from castes, *we may find our own healing*, a beloved society in which there is neither Jew nor Greek, slave nor free, male or female, straight, gay, or transgender, black, brown, or white, *but all walks of life as one community.* This would be the kind of community that Jesus envisioned, and this would be a radical response to the divisiveness that is so prevalent in our country today. And by becoming this kind of community in our divided world, we may be able to address the discouragement and negative criticism that so many of the "nones" and "dones" feel toward religious institutions.

Some of the most discouraging polls for religious leaders serving religious institutions and conducted by such respected organizations as Gallup and Pew are those recent polls showing that the fastest-growing group of persons when asked about their religious affiliation are the "nones" and "dones." These are persons who do not want to be affiliated with any religious denomination and those who have completely left their religious institutions, never to return. The Quakers have a phrase they use when they are pleased with something: They say, "That speaks to my condition." Unfortunately, for the "nones" and "dones," the church, in any of its varied forms, *does not* speak to their condition.

In 2013, Joani and Thom Schultz published a book titled *Why Nobody Wants to Go to Church Anymore.* In August 2021, Dr. Steve McSwain wrote an article with the same title. He quotes a Hartford Institute for Religion Research report that says 40 percent of Americans say they go to church weekly. He writes that the truth is, "20% are actually in church." The article raises some important issues about why people are no longer going to church. McSwain points to the changing demographics of America, as well as new technology, the competition of various activities on Sunday, and the leadership crisis, on which he blames the clergy abuse scandal and fundamentalist preachers who drive people away with their threatening language. (Nobody wants to be told one is facing eternal damnation.) He also says that phony advertising is driving people away. Churches advertise that "everyone is welcome," but this is not true. The Millennials can see right through this lie. McSwain points out that eight thousand to ten thousand churches will likely close this year, and that each year nearly three million previous churchgoers enter the ranks of the religiously unaffiliated.[10]

In the Pew Research Center–sponsored study "Why America's 'nones' left religion behind," Michael Lipka writes, "About half of current 'nones' who were raised in a religion (49%) indicate that a lack of belief led them to move away from religion. This includes many respondents who mention 'science' as the reason they do not believe in religious teachings." The author continues, "But there are other reasons people give for leaving behind their childhood religion. One in five express an opposition to organized religion in general. This share includes some who do not like the hierarchical nature of religious groups, several people who think religion is too much like a business and others who mention clergy sexual abuse scandals as reasons for their stance." Other reasons include these:

- "Too many Christians doing un-Christian things."
- "Rational thought makes religion go out the window."
- "Lack of any sort of scientific or specific evidence of a creator."

The dislike of organized religion drew the following responses:

- "I see organized religious groups as more divisive than uniting."
- "I think that more harm has been done in the name of religion than any other area."
- "I no longer believe in organized religion. I don't attend services anymore. It's a business. It's all about money."
- "The clergy sex abuse scandal."
- "The church's teaching on homosexuality."[11]

Another Pew Research Center report states,

We recently asked a representative sample of more than 1,300 of these 'nones' why they choose not to identify with a religion. Out of several options included in the survey, the most common reason they give is that they question a lot of religious teachings.

Six in ten religiously unaffiliated Americans—adults who describe their religious identity as atheist, agnostic or 'nothing in particular'—say the questioning of religious teachings is a very important reason for their lack of affiliation. The second most common reason is opposition to the positions taken by churches on social and political issues, cited by 49% of respondents. Smaller, but a still substantial group says they dislike religious organizations (41%), don't believe in God (37%), consider religion irrelevant to them (36%) or dislike religious leaders (34%).[12]

In so many cases, there is nothing that the church and its religious leaders can do to convince the "nones" and "dones" to return to the religious institutions they have left, or to convince them to enter an institution where they have never darkened the door. Perhaps there will be a crisis, the loss of a loved one or another worldwide calamity, that will cause them to return to the best-prepared institution that can offer them comfort and hope. I don't know. I am convinced, however, that there are some things religious leaders can do to adjust to the new institutional landscape that is rapidly developing.

First of all, I believe that we will not attract the seekers of today by becoming more like the culture that surrounds us. I do not think that more entertainment within our houses of worship will bring the transformation that is currently needed. Our problems run much deeper than what a good band and praise song can cure. In an op-ed for the *New York Times*, David Brooks wrote an article titled "America Is Falling Apart at the Seams." After several examples, many of which have already been noted about what is going *wrong* in our country, Brooks writes, "It has to be said that not every trend is bad. Substance use among teenagers, for example, seems to be declining. And a lot of these problems are caused by the presumably temporary stress of the pandemic. I doubt as many people would be punching flight attendants or throwing temper tantrums over cheese if there weren't mask rules and a deadly virus to worry about.

"*But something darker and deeper seems to be happening as well—a long-term loss of solidarity, a long-term rise in estrangement and hostility. This is what it feels like to live in a society that is dissolving from the bottom up as much as from the top down.*

"*What the hell is going on? The short answer: I don't know*"[13] (italics added).

Our problems, I am convinced, are not material, although there are those in our society who are living on the edge, many not knowing where their next meal is coming from. Instead, I suggest that our problems, at base, are *spiritual*. We are trying to live through and respond to the various problems with which we are confronted, without a spiritual compass. The sustaining roots of any civilization are spiritual, and religious leaders need to keep reminding us that if we try to live together without a spiritual base, we will wither and die.

A while back, I was present at a luncheon at which the featured speaker was Thomas Cahill, the celebrated author of *How the Irish Saved Civilization*. At the conclusion of his presentation, I asked him this question: "All other civilizations have declined and eventually died. What gives you hope that ours will survive?" His quick response: "I am not at all sure that it will survive!" Later, I finished reading his famous book, and read how he believes our civilization *may* survive. He writes:

As we the people of the first world, the Romans of the twentieth-century, look out across our Earth, we see some signs for hope, many more for despair. Technology proceeds apace, delivering the marvels that knit our world together—the conquering of diseases that plagued every age but ours and the consequent lowering of mortality rates, revolutions in crop yields that continue to feed expanding populations, the internet that enables all of us to retrieve information and communicate with one another in ways so instant and complete that they would dazzle those who built the Roman roads, the first great information system.

But the road system became impassable rubble, as the empire was overwhelmed by population explosions beyond its borders. So will ours. Rome's demise instructs us in what inevitably happens when impoverished and rapidly expanding populations, whose ways and values are dimly understood, press up against a rich and ordered society. More than a billion people in our world today survive on less than $370.00 a year. . . . If the world's population, which has doubled in our lifetime, doubles again by the middle of this century, how could anyone hope to escape the catastrophic consequences—the wrath to come?

What will be lost, and what saved, of our civilization probably lies beyond our powers to decide. No human group has ever figured out how to design its future." And then, after Cahill outlines the problems we are facing, he offers us a peek into how we might be saved: "That future may be germinating today not in a boardroom in London or an office in Washington, or a bank in Tokyo, but in some antic outpost or other—a kindly British orphanage in the grim foothills of Peru, a house for the dying in a back street of Calcutta, a mission to Somalia by Irish social workers who remember their own Great Hunger—in some unheralded corner where a great hearted human being is committed to loving outcasts in an extraordinary way. . . . If our civilization is to be saved—forget about our civilization, which as Saint Patrick would say, may pass 'in a moment like a cloud or smoke that is scattered by the wind'—*if we are to be saved, it will not be by Romans, but by saints.*[14] (italics added)

While I was serving as the minister of faith and learning at Wayzata Community Church in Minnesota, I invited Karen Armstrong, the former nun and now prolific author, to speak about her book *The Great Transformation: The Beginning of Our Religious Traditions.* Of the many important points that she made, none seemed more important than this: "Compassion is the wellspring of religion." She observed that some five hundred years before Jesus, Confucius expressed the Golden Rule. It remains the touchstone of all the major faith traditions. Compassion, Armstrong said is, "a concern for the sufferings and misfortunes of others." Living together requires us to have a concern for others. We are no longer a culture that is *only* Christian. We are a culture filled with many kinds of spiritual traditions as well as a large group that does not profess any religious tradition. When Karen Armstrong was asked by an audience participant what we can do to help bring together the multiple faith groups that are part of America, she responded, "We should not talk about what we believe. We must go beyond tolerance and dialogue and *work* together. We must let our actions show what we believe, what we hold in common." To work together in our communities of diversity, showing what compassion looks like and what our faith looks like in practical ways that truly help people, is to respond in a positive way to many of the problems that we are facing in today's new world, and by our practical actions of love and caring, the "nones" and the "dones" may want to join us.

Earlier in this chapter, I quoted a Facebook post by Anne Lamott in which she shared what she was feeling as we began our third year in the pandemic. She said that she felt she was *done*, just *done*. This feeling of hopelessness was not the end of her post. She went on to write, "So now what?" Her friend Tom W. wrote to her, "'We remember to remember.' And that's the answer. We remember that we are alive. We remember the old tried and true things that always bless us—gather if we can, pay gentle attention to others, get outside even in the cold and wet, send money to the poor and to NPR. We remember to give thanks that, after so much has been taken from us, so many blessings remain. . . . We say thanks over and over for everything that still works, all that we still love. . . . Gratitude is the fountain of youth. It's soul food—chicken and waffles and peach cobbler. It's magnetized. We remember that spring will be here soon, proving every year that life is stronger than death, than all of the chaos. . . . Today I will remember what my priest friend Terry says, that the point is not to try harder but to resist less; and I will remember that grace finds us exactly where we are but does not leave us where it found us. . . . I remember how so many of you have been here and with me through it all, and that has made all of the difference. So, thank you . . . thank you."[15]

Notes

1. Brogdon, Lewis. "The Fight for the Soul of America." *Christian Ethics Today*, Summer 2021.

2. Camus, Albert. *The Plague*. New York: Vintage Books, 1975.

3. Lamott, Anne. Facebook page, January, 2022. www.facebook.com/Anne Lamott.

4. Wright, N. T. *God and the Pandemic: A Christian Reflection on the Coronavirus and Its Aftermath*. Grand Rapids: Zondervan, 2020.

5. https://www.cnn.com/2020/06/30/health/us-coronavirus-toll-in-numbers-june-trnd/index.html.

6. "MSF's response to Covid-19 in the United States." Medecins Sans Frontiers, April 17, 2020. https://www.doctorswithoutborders.org/latest/faq-msfs-covid-19-response-united-states.

7. EquaSion. "A *Mighty Stream* Discussion Guide on Race and Racial Equity." 2022.

8. Jones, Robert P. *White Too Long: The Legacy of White Supremacy in American Christianity.* New York: Simon and Schuster, 2020.

9. Wilkerson, Isabel. *Caste: The Origins of Our Discontents.* New York: Random House, 2020.

10. McSwain, Steve. "Why Nobody Wants to Go to Church Anymore." *Beliefnet,* August 16, 2021. https://www.beliefnet.com/faiths/galleries/why-nobody-wants-to-go-to-church-anymore.aspx.

11. Lipka, Michael. "Why America's 'nones' left religion behind." Pew Research Center, August 24, 2016. https://www.pewresearch.org/fact-tank/2016/08/24/why-americas-nones-left-religion-behind/.

12. Pew Research Center. "Why America's 'nones' don't identify with a religion." August 8, 2018. https://www.pewresearch.org/fact-tank/2018/08/08/why-americas-nones-dont-identify-with-a-religion/.

13. Brooks, David. "America Is Falling Apart at the Seams." *New York Times,* January 13, 2022.

14. Cahill, Thomas. *How the Irish Saved Civilization: The Untold Story of Ireland's Heroic Role from the Fall of Rome to the Rise of Medieval Europe.* New York: Anchor Books, 1995.

15. Lamott, Anne. Facebook post, January 22, 2022.

7

~

Building Trust within a
Culture of Mistrust

Are you finding ways to build trust and nurture community, even as religious insti-
tutions face political and doctrinal division? How are you addressing the issues sur-
rounding gender inclusivity and ethnic diversity? How are you making the internal
adjustments to the outward changes in culture?

I recently watched, in brief, a political rally in Ohio that was promoted
by former president Trump. By anyone's standards of civility, it was very
disconcerting, or a more appropriate descriptive word would be "vulgar."
There were people yelling obscenities and lifting their middle fingers at the
press. There were the Make America Great Again hats and shirts that one
has come to expect at such rallies, as well as placards expressing their distrust
of vaccines and masks. All in all, it was difficult to watch, and so, after a few
minutes, I quit watching.

At the outset of this chapter, I want to share that I understand the frustration and anger of the rally attendees. For several years, our country has been
going through a time of distrust . . . distrust of the press, distrust of Congress,
distrust of banks, distrust of the public school system, and because of recent
decisions, distrust of the Supreme Court. It is not an exaggeration to say that
a large swath of our country no longer believes that the institutions that have
had as their main purpose to uphold our civilization are no longer working
for the common person.

In an article for *National Journal* titled "In Nothing We Trust," Ron Fournier
and Sophie Quinton focus on my hometown of Muncie, Indiana. In sociological studies, especially the famous Lynd studies, Muncie is often referred
to as "Middletown USA." The article includes an interview with a man
who had lost his job, his wife lost her job, and his home had been foreclosed
upon because the modification that he had worked out with the bank was

canceled, and he could not come up with the $1,800 in back payments the bank said he owed. This man felt betrayed and cut adrift by a society that no longer valued him. He became a supporter of President Trump, believing that Trump might be the answer to many of his financial woes as well as his low self-esteem.

The statistics in this article mirror the feelings of the man who had lost his job and home: seven in ten Americans believe that the country is on the wrong track. Eight in ten are dissatisfied with the way the nation is being governed. Only 23 percent have confidence in banks and just 19 percent have confidence in big business. Less than half of the population expresses a great deal of confidence in the public school system *or organized religion.* "We have lost our gods," the article quotes Laura Hansen, a professor of sociology, as saying. "We have lost faith in the media. . . . We have lost faith in our culture. . . . We have lost a sense of trust and confidence in everything." Professor Hansen continues,

> When people trust their institutions, they are better able to solve common problems. Research shows that school principals are much more likely to turn around struggling schools in places where people have a history of working together and getting involved in their children's education. Communities bonded by friendships formed at religious institutions are more likely to vote, volunteer, and perform everyday good deeds like helping someone find a job. And governments find it easier to persuade the public to make sacrifices for the common good when people trust their political leaders to have the community's best interests at heart.[1]

A loss of trust in our society has been a long time coming, but former president Trump's continued focus on spreading "The Big Lie" (that the 2020 election was rigged, and he should still be president) is accentuating this loss of trust and threatening our democracy. We are in a downward spiral of lies and violence. We are now living in a society of alternative realities and misinformation, and this phenomenon has not stopped at the doors of our churches. In an article for *Axios* titled "QAnon infects churches," Mike Allen writes, "QAnon conspiracy theories have burrowed so deeply into American churches that pastors are expressing alarm. A new poll shows that bogus teachings have become widespread. . . . The problem with misinformation and disinformation is that people—lots of people— believe it. And they don't believe reality coming from the media and even their ministers." This poll showed that 15 percent of Americans agree with the QAnon contention that "the government, media, and financial worlds in the U.S. are controlled by a group of Satan-worshipping pedophiles who run a global child sex trafficking operation."[2] (*Ipsos poll* taken for the *Public Religion Research Institute*)[3]

On a personal note, I am not unfamiliar with political delusion. It is not the kind of crazy delusion that we are experiencing today, but still it was delusion. My grandmother, who was a teetotaling conservative Quaker, operated within a delusion surrounding former president Richard Nixon, putting him on a very high pedestal. I was with my grandmother when Nixon made his historic trip to communist China. In the news footage about the trip, it showed Nixon and the president of China sharing a toast of white wine at dinner. Seeing an opportunity to tease my grandmother, I said, "Look, Grandma! Our Quaker president drinking wine!" Her quick response, "Oh, no. President Nixon is just letting the wine touch his lips, he is not swallowing!" It is easy to lose sight of reality when we worship our political leaders.

"This Is Not What I Signed Up For" reads the headline of an article on ChurchLeaders.com, followed by "Unsettling Exodus of Pastors Leaving the Ministry." Dan White Jr. of the KINEO Center, a place focused on offering healing for tired and traumatized leaders, asked himself in the article, "What is occurring?" This exodus is not centered in any one or two denominations but is from a mix, including Baptist, Lutheran, Anglican, Methodist, and Mennonite. White says, "I've been coaching for about 10 years, and I have never seen this kind of disruption." Christopher B. James, a professor at the University of Dubuque Theological Seminary, said, "In addition to being a hard job with mediocre pay, many pastors don't think it is worth it to try to maintain dying churches and are curious what Christian life and leadership might look like outside the clergy role. It's part of a wider unraveling and reconfiguration of church." A former pastor wrote, "After 30 years I felt God was calling me out of paid ministry into the marketplace. I'm convinced that many, many pastors have lost the ability to speak the same language of those outside the church." Another minister shared, "Since the pandemic started, it's never been harder to be a pastor. People are less committed than ever, people are angry, if you make a stand for Jesus that doesn't fit with people's favorite news station they'll attempt a coup, finances are down, and we are overworked with little to no thanks."[4]

For many religious leaders, the exodus from the institution began before the pandemic. A few years ago, Barbara Brown Taylor wrote a book titled *Leaving Church: A Memoir of Faith*. In it she describes her leaving the Episcopal priesthood and starting a whole new life. There were many reasons why she left, including spiritual burnout, some depression, and life changes that moved her to reconsider what she was doing. In her final chapter, called "Keeping," Taylor writes:

For most of my adult life, what I have wanted most to win is nearness to God. This led me to choose a vocation that marked me as God's person both in my eyes and in the eyes of others. I gave myself to the work the best way I knew how, which sometimes exhausted my parishioners as much as it exhausted me. I thought that being faithful meant always trying harder to live a holier life and calling them to do the same. I thought that it meant knowing everything I could about scripture and theology and showing up every time the church doors were open, and never saying no to anyone in need. I thought it meant ignoring my own needs and those of my family until they went away all together, leaving me free to serve God without any selfish desires to drag me down.

I thought that being faithful was about becoming someone other than who I was, in other words, and it was not until this project failed that I began to wonder if my human wholeness might be more useful to God than my exhausting goodness.[5]

Many of us who have given our lives to ministry know the feelings behind the words that Barbara Brown Taylor writes. I know personally what "exhausting goodness" feels like, and if you are a religious leader, so do you. A few paragraphs later in this same chapter in *Leaving Church*, she tells us what beyond the religious institution is saving her life now: "Teaching school is saving my life now. . . . Living in relationship with creation is saving my life now. . . . Observing the Sabbath is saving my life now. . . . Encountering God is saving my life now. . . . Committing myself to the task of becoming fully human is saving my life now."[6]

There is a great resignation going on in this country. In an article titled "Why Pastors Are Joining the Great Resignation," Melissa Florer-Bixler writes,

The Great Resignation is underway in the United States with an astounding 3 percent of employees collectively refusing the terms of low-wages, absent benefits, and dangerous working conditions expected by their bosses. Pastors, too, are walking away. Recent poll data collected by Barna Group, a California-based research firm that studies faith and culture, confirmed what I'm seeing among my friends and colleagues. According to Barna, about 38% of Protestant senior pastors surveyed have considered leaving ministry over the past year. Among pastors under age 45, that number rose to 46%.

In her own survey, Florer-Bixler learned why many are leaving: "An intractable conflict. Embedded sexism. Shifting congregational commitments. Unclear paths for ministry following the pandemic. Exhaustion, low pay, and lack of appreciation."[7]

These reasons for leaving have all been expressed by our *Sacred Chaos* participants.

And, of course, the divisions caused by what is being labeled as "Trumpian politics" are also contributing to the exodus of religious leaders from the church. Florer-Bixler continues,

> But in the wreckage of Trumpian politics and a never-ending pandemic, our jobs have been reduced to negotiating skirmishes over mask-wearing and vaccination status. Former and current pastors have shared with me that their denominations and powerful congregants have pushed for a false unity that tolerates homophobia, racism and conspiracy theories. My friend Ryan, a seasoned pastor, finally gave up. He felt that he could no longer follow the work of the Holy Spirit when he was expected to make room for people who actively thwarted God's movement. When we name the need to repent of sexism and racism, powerful church members withhold their giving and muster factions to oust us. Our compassion fatigue is real.[8]

Add to these concerns the splits that are occurring in denomination after denomination. A friend of mine, a Southern Baptist minister, once told me what it felt like when the Southern Baptists went through their time of purging the denomination of what some felt were heretics and false teachers. During the three-year fundamentalist move toward taking the denomination over, he said, the first year was like he was a pallbearer at the cemetery, walking the casket of the Southern Baptist denomination to the grave. The second year he felt like he was standing over the grave as the casket was lowered, and then he took shovelfuls of dirt to throw on top of it. The third year, he said, it felt like he was slowly walking away from the grave, weeping. I am sure that many within the United Methodist Church are feeling this same way as the church works toward a split over the issue of marriage equality and the ordination of gay clergy.

Mary is a minister within the United Methodist Church. Her personal chaos is fueled by the chaos within her denomination as it splits into camps over the issues just described.

Mary was aware of this developing chasm for many years, and more intensely in recent years. She was experiencing the tensions of growing up in a rural, and consequently more conservative, community, and yet upon completing seminary, with her mind and heart expanded, she felt deeply about inclusivity and critical thinking (i.e., the cultural context of when Scripture was written and the history of how the church has interpreted Scripture over the years). She could see the fundamental issue as to how one approaches Scripture—the literal interpretation of her upbringing where she still feels strongly connected to family and friends versus the critical, more progressive approach she learned in seminary. Mary continued to believe that love would bind the church—the United Methodist Church—together. As the UMC faced a likely realignment over the issue of human sexuality—specifically over whether LGBTQ members could be ordained or married within the blessing of the institution—she continued to hope for some middle ground, a pathway on which they could all remain together. She felt that each congregation could make its own determinations about these matters. If the UMC splits into two different branches of the Wesleyan tradition, it will feel terribly painful to Mary as she would likely join the progressive church. She also worried that if a split took place, there would be many more progressive ministers looking for congregations to serve than would be available within her conference. She was beginning to experience the grief of the estrangement within her church that would forever change her relationships.

All of us who are religious leaders today feel the pain of these separations, the estrangement that Mary was feeling. Every mainline denomination, including the orthodox branch of Quakerism, has been through this. The main issues causing such separations are, as just mentioned in reference to the United Methodist Church, whether to ordain clergy who are openly gay, as well as support marriage equality. And then there is this *oldie* but *goodie* still relevant today: "Do you believe the Bible is *literally* true?" What we are experiencing is painful. Is it possible, during this time of record numbers of religious leaders resigning and in this time of values confusion and mistrust in our society and in the church, that we can learn to agree to differ, resolve to love, and unite in ministry? I don't know. I hope so. I am reminded of my own experience of living in a home in which we disagreed with one another politically but in the end resolved to love one another. It was a different time, to be sure, but many of the same underlying issues of disagreement that are present now were present then.

My father thought that Hubert Humphrey was one of the greatest men who ever lived. He had worked with then-mayor Humphrey in the 1950s, serving with him on the human-relations council in Minneapolis. Ever since, he had followed with great interest Humphrey's political career. I did not know the Hubert Humphrey prior to his time as vice president under President Lyndon B. Johnson. And I was not nearly as fond of him as my father was. I was a freshman in college in 1968 when Humphrey decided to run for the presidency.

Also running for president was a Minnesota senator named Eugene McCarthy. I liked him in 1968. He represented a change from the past and was popular with young people. As these men debated the Vietnam War and other important issues, they also set the stage for a debate in our family. To make things even more interesting, my grandmother, who was living with us at the time, was an ardent supporter of Richard Nixon. After all, he was a Quaker, and my grandmother felt that we should support "one of our own." Our home was not a pleasant place to eat dinner. Inevitably, someone would raise the subject of politics each time we sat down at the table together.

"And for this food, we give Thee thanks. Amen." "Dad, did you hear what McCarthy said today?" "I heard that Richard Nixon has a secret plan to end the war." "If we just let Hubert run his own show, he will be a terrific president." I am not sure of the order of such comments, but they were all there. From the moment the prayer of thanksgiving ended until the last bite of dessert, politics dominated mealtime.

As I reflect on those family meals, I cannot help but smile. There we were, one middle-class family carrying the weight of the world's problems on our shoulders. We really did love one another beyond our differing political beliefs, and I suppose that during such times together I learned how to differ with someone over religion or politics while at the same time respecting and loving the person behind the belief. Many years later, I read the words of Robert Owen, founder of a socialist community in New Harmony, Indiana, and remembered those dinner discussions: "If we cannot reconcile all opinions, let us endeavor to unite all hearts." This is not to say that our verbal exchanges did not skirt the boundary of human respect. They did. In the end, however, we knew that we were still family, and that our hearts were united in love.

Unfortunately, we have reached a point where we no longer listen to one another but instead see who can debate his or her point of view the most loudly. Talk radio and cable news are famous for this kind of lack of civility, but it has infiltrated all segments of our lives. Our problems are beyond being Republican or Democrat, Baptist, Roman Catholic, or Methodist. The problems are *spiritual*. We care more about winning a discussion or argument than about the person with the different point of view.

Dehumanizing someone or some group that we do not know is temptingly easy. I recently shared a post on Facebook about immigrants, dispelling the untruths that have been circulating and challenging the negative words that have recently been used against them. (A candidate for the Senate in Ohio is running an advertisement that says of immigrants, "They are coming to our country for the *freebies*, spreading disease and taking your jobs.") Here is one of the responses I received from a friend I knew in high school: "The truth about immigrants—whenever anyone begins a sentence with 'The Truth' I immediately become suspect of what is to follow—legal or not, is that they bring diseases back to America that have been eradicated for years. Most turn to a life of crime because they do not speak English. If a person wants to live in America, they should learn English." A commentator on Fox News could not have said it better. I am reminded of the comedian Chris Rock, who was commenting on the Republican National Convention's decision to put an "English only" provision in its platform. The Convention was meeting in San Diego. Rock said, "Look at where we are meeting! *San Diego!*" My response to my high school friend was simple: "My wife is a Latina migrant." We can all think of times we would like to take back our hurtful words or Facebook posts. I am sure that my friend from high school had no idea that I had married a Hispanic migrant woman, and if he could change his reply to my post he probably would. What we say matters. Words matter. Today our rhetoric has reached a new level of harshness and meanness.

I first became acquainted with M. Scott Peck (Scotty to his friends) when he led seminars on his books at the Yokefellow Institute on the back campus of Earlham College. He is mostly known for his best seller *The Road Less Traveled*, but it was his book on civility, *A World Waiting to Be Born: Civility Rediscovered*, that most interested me. Scotty was very concerned about the deteriorating state of civility in our society, and so he worked on developing some ways that we can discuss religion and politics in a *civil way*.[9] He believed that civility could be renewed in our society, unlike Samuel Johnson, who wrote, "When once the forms of civility are violated there remains little hope of return to kindness and decency."[10] Scotty sought to disprove Johnson's statement.

In a Scott Peck–sponsored seminar on civility that I attended, we interacted with one another, telling our stories. We talked about the major faith events in our lives that were teachable or awakening. We discussed the political events that shaped us. Instead of asking, "*What* do you believe?" we asked one another, "*Why* do you believe?" In the two days of the seminar, we came to understand one another in a civilized way, rather than hurling our points of view at one another.

To share with one another in a civil way, certain elements must underlie our life together. The first element is *trust*. Perhaps the most trusting figure in American popular culture is Charlie Brown, the comic strip character created by Charles Schulz. Those familiar with Charlie Brown and the *Peanuts* characters can remember the many episodes featuring Charlie Brown, Lucy, and a football. Lucy challenges Charlie Brown to kick the ball while she holds it. Charlie is sure that Lucy will pull the ball away just as he tries to kick it, and he will end up flat on his back. He says to her,

"You must think I am crazy. You say that you will hold the ball, but you won't. You will pull it away and I'll break my neck." With the look of an angel, Lucy responds with a wide smile, "Why Charlie Brown, how you talk! I wouldn't think of such a thing. I am a changed person. Look, isn't this the face of a person you can trust?" Since Charlie Brown is Charlie Brown, he accepts Lucy at her word. "All right, you hold the ball and I'll come running up and kick it." Sure enough, the expected happens, and as Charlie flies to the ground, he can only shout, "She did it again!" In the last scene, Lucy is leaning over Charlie to say, "I admire you, Charlie Brown. You have such faith in human nature."

In a sense, our whole society is built on the kind of trust that Charlie Brown displays. Civility is not possible without trust, even though such trust may at times be misplaced.

The art of *listening* also is important to civil discourse, within both our religious institutions and our society at large. During this Scott Peck seminar, two or three of us sat together and listened to one another. Each person had three minutes to speak, and the rule was that no one could interrupt. This is not as easy as it sounds! In our era of talking at one another and short attention spans, patient, attentive listening to one another is a very difficult discipline. And yet, if we are to recover civility in our interactions with one another, it is an absolute necessity.

Another element helpful in the recovery of civility is *vulnerability*. Being open and vulnerable, letting our defenses down as we interact with one another, will help us be more civil, and it will help us grow spiritually. The more open and vulnerable we become, and the more authentic we can be with one another, the more civil our discourse will be.

Vulnerability. It is a word that takes on more and more spiritual meaning as we mature, especially if such maturing involves experiencing some chaos in our lives. Experiencing change and moving from one chapter of life to another, we will confront new ways that challenge our old ways of thinking and our well-ordered patterns of living. As uncomfortable as being vulnerable makes us, it is the passageway to becoming closer to God, a God who is continuously taking risks and becoming vulnerable to stay connected to us. In our vulnerable discomfort, God opens our hearts and challenges us to explore new possibilities. The more open and vulnerable we become, the more authentic we can be with others, the more we will grow spiritually, and the more intimate our relationships will be with others. The author Madeleine L'Engle has written, "When we were children, we used to think that when we were grown-up we would no longer be vulnerable. But to grow-up is to accept vulnerability. To be alive is to be vulnerable."[11]

In a very practical way, we can practice trusting, listening, and becoming vulnerable in what Quakers call threshing meetings. In the Britain Yearly Meeting's *Quaker Faith and Practice*, one of these meetings is described: "This term currently denotes a meeting at which a variety of different, and sometimes controversial, opinions can be openly, and sometimes forcefully, expressed, often in order to defuse a situation before a later meeting for worship for business."[12] No decisions are made in threshing meetings. They only serve as venues for people who disagree to vent their concerns. A clerk, someone who is not biased and who is trusted and respected by all persons representing various sides of the issue, is chosen to keep the discussion civil and loving. I have personally witnessed these meetings in action, and I am very impressed by the way they give all persons present an opportunity to express themselves, as well as give all persons an opportunity to listen to others. These types of meetings are especially helpful if conducted before business meetings during which difficult decisions must be made.

On the wall in my study hangs the motto of Plymouth Congregational Church in Des Moines, Iowa. It reads: "We agree to differ . . . We resolve to love . . . We unite to serve." These words are part of a larger saying that was displayed above the door of the ashram in India of the American missionary E. Stanley Jones: "Here we enter a fellowship. Sometimes we will agree to differ, but always we will resolve to love and unite to serve." A community of faith, a denomination, a society that agrees to differ but resolves to love one another will be a community incorporating the elements of *trust, listening,* and *vulnerability*. At times we will fail. In so many respects today we are failing, but then, if we are to survive, we begin again. To live together requires nothing less.

It may have been over two thousand years ago, but it was also very much like the time in which we are now living. There was a growing gap between the very rich and the poor. Those under occupied Roman rule lacked trust in traditional institutions, with religious leaders collaborating with the occupying force of Rome. Those in Roman leadership showed a lack of concern for those persons society considered disposable, the "under the bridge" dwellers of that day. Politicians in Rome argued over matters that rarely helped or affected the general population, and people suspected anyone in authority.

In his novel *Doctor Zhivago*, Boris Pasternak writes about Roman culture and the way Jesus changed that culture:

> Rome was a flea market of borrowed gods and conquered peoples, a bargain
> basement on two floors, earth and heaven, a mass of filth convoluted in a
> triple knot as in an intestinal obstruction. Dacians, Herulians, Scythians,

Sarmatians, Hyperboreans, heavy wheels without spokes, illiterate emperors, fish fed on the flesh of learned slaves . . . all crammed into the passages of the Coliseum, and all wretched.

And then, into this tasteless heap of gold and marble, He came, light and clothed in an aura, emphatically human, deliberately provincial Galilean, and at that moment gods and nations ceased to be and humans came into being.[13] (italics added)

Like all religious leaders, I am trying to understand and do ministry in the time in which we are now living. The angry political rallies, the distrust of institutions, the fear, the sexism and racism, the splits in churches and denominations over marriage equality and gay clergy, and the ever-present split over how to interpret Scripture. As a result of trying to understand and search for responses to these various issues, I find myself at a place, in the words of theologian Marcus Borg, where I am seeking to "meet Jesus again for the first time" and understand the radical love that surrounded his life. How might the life and teachings of Jesus give us hope today and help us build trust within our culture of mistrust?

I believe that through the centuries, Jesus has attracted so many to himself because of his understanding that God *is love*. In his book *Unlearning God*, Philip Gulley has written: "So God is love, right? Well, that depends on how we understand love. I'm reluctant to ascribe human emotions to God, as if God were an extrapolation of humanity. . . . I believe that God is that essence in us that reaches out to another, committed to their well-being, their enlightenment, their moral, emotional, relational, and spiritual growth."[14] Jesus embodied this kind of love in his own life in a radical way that gave his life its richness and ultimate meaning. This kind of love also lies at the base of how we begin to rebuild trust of one another in a society of mistrust.

Building trust based on the radical love that Jesus represented will take an intentional effort on behalf of the leaders in our society to make life more equitable. We can no longer afford the luxury of a tax system that rewards the wealthy and penalizes the middle and lower classes of society. The gap between the very rich and the very poor continues to grow, and the destructive impact on our society because of this gap is very harmful. I once heard Jim Wallis of *Sojourners* remark that archaeologists in Israel have learned that when the wealth gap was the greatest in ancient Israel, the prophets were the most active.

Jesus had a remarkable ability to communicate with the "throwaways" of our society, like the man in Muncie, Indiana, who had lost his job and his house. For people living in distrust of their institutions and living on the edges of their society, imagine what it must have been like to listen to the words "Blessed are the poor in spirit. . . . Blessed are those who mourn. . . . Blessed are the meek. . . . Blessed are those who hunger and thirst for righteousness. . . . Blessed are the peacemakers. . . . Blessed are those who are persecuted for righteousness' sake. . . . Blessed are you when others revile you and persecute you and utter all kinds of evil against you falsely on my account" (Matthew 5:3–6, 9–11). It most surely gave the people living on the edges of society in Jesus's time a great feeling of hope. *Inclusivity* was the hope of that day, and it is the hopeful word for our day . . . gender inclusivity, however one defines one's gender, and ethnic diversity, the acceptance of everyone regardless of ethnic background. This is America, and this is what today's church should reflect. It is certainly the kind of world that Jesus envisioned.

Father Gregory Boyle in his book *Tattoos on the Heart: The Power of Boundless Compassion* describes what an all-inclusive community would look like:

> Only kinship. Inching ourselves closer to creating a community of kinship such that God might recognize it. Soon we imagine, with God, this circle of compassion. Then we imagine no one standing outside of that circle, moving ourselves closer to the margins so that the margins themselves will be erased. We stand there with those whose dignity has been denied. We locate ourselves with the poor and the powerless and the voiceless. At the edges, we join the easily despised and the readily left out. We stand with the demonized so that the demonizing will stop. We situate ourselves right next to the disposable so that the day will come when we stop throwing people away.[15]

A major task for religious leaders today is to work toward that day *when we stop throwing people away*. I am convinced that when *we situate ourselves right next to the disposable*, we will begin the process of building trust within a culture of mistrust. This is the kind of love in action that Jesus envisioned about human community. This vision was formed from his experience of a God of love, and as his followers, this is what we are to be about.

The building of trust within a culture of mistrust is the responsibility of all persons. This responsibility, however, weighs heavily upon religious leaders. To where else in our society do people turn for hope and counsel during these untrusting times? Who else will share the vision that Jesus had for an all-inclusive community? The religious leader and the institution he or she serves must answer the call for inclusivity, or the institution as we know it will only mirror the divisions in our society and will eventually die. Many religious leaders will not be able to withstand the pushback to such a model of diversity and will, to the detriment of the Christian community, leave their churches. Transitional times make for painful discussions and painful decisions. Such difficult discussions and decisions, however, are necessary if we are to have a relevant future.

Notes

1. Fournier, Ron and Sophie Quinton. "In Nothing We Trust." *The Atlantic*, April 12, 2012.

2. Allen, Mike. "QAnon infects churches." *Axios*, May 31, 2021. https://www.axios.com/2021/05/31/qanon-churches-popular-religion-conspiracy-theory.

3. Ipsos Poll. Public Religion Research Institute, as quoted in "QAnon Infects the Church" by Mike Allen.

4. Jackson, Jesse T. "This Is Not What I Signed Up For." *ChurchLeaders.com*, May 7, 2021. https://churchleaders.com/news/396413-reports-of-an-unsettling-trend-of-pastors-leaving-the-ministry.html.

5. Taylor, Barbara Brown. *Leaving Church: A Memoir of Faith*. San Francisco: HarperSanFrancisco, 2006.

6. Ibid.

7. Florer-Bixler, Melissa. "Why Pastors Are Joining the Great Resignation." *Sojourners*, November 30, 2021.

8. Ibid.

9. Peck, M. Scott. *A World Waiting to Be Born: Civility Rediscovered*. New York: Bantam Books, 1993.

10. Johnson, Samuel. *The Rambler, Number 55*. Charleson, South Carolina: Nabu Press, 2012.

11. L'Engle, Madeleine. www.guideposts.org.

12. Britain Yearly Meeting. *Quaker Faith and Practice*. Warwick: Warwick Printing Company, 1995.

13. Pasternak, Boris. *Doctor Zhivago*. Pantheon, 1957.

14. Gulley, Philip. *Unlearning God: How Unbelieving Helped Me Believe*. New York: Convergent Books, 2018.

15. Boyle, Gregory. *Tattoos on the Heart: The Power of Boundless Compassion*. New York: Simon and Schuster, 2010.

8

~

The Recovery of Certain Virtues

What virtues need to be recovered? What is the role of religious leaders in the recovery of certain virtues? Do you understand that an important part of the role of a religious leader is to speak the truth to power?

The following words have been attributed to Stephen Grellet, "I expect to pass through this world but once; any good thing therefore that I can do, or any kindness that I can show to any fellow creature, let me do it now; let me not defer or neglect it, for I shall not pass this way again." It is a clarion call for religious leaders . . . *do it now.* I submit that one of the most important, good, and kind things religious leaders can do today is help renew certain virtues that our world has lost or is losing. It will, on occasion, mean speaking truth to the powerful forces of the status quo, and yet if renewal of our society and communities of faith is to be, then such truth-speaking is necessary.

The first virtue that we need to recover is courage. It was Robert Louis Stevenson who said, "Courage is the primary virtue because all of the others presuppose it." At first glance, and perhaps at second and third glances as well, this does not seem to be a very courageous time. It is more a time of cautious expediency. To believe in what you believe . . . being totally authentic . . . without the fear of the consequences, is to live in a spirit of courage. Those persons we most admire are those who have stood for the right, even though all around them are criticizing them for it. In the immediate moment, it might not be politically expedient to take a certain position because of the flak one will receive, but if that position is true, and if it is right, and if it is just, the courageous individual will be willing to accept the consequences now for the goal of justice in the future. It was Martin Luther King Jr. who said, "The arc of the moral universe is long, but it bends toward justice."

The second virtue that needs to be recovered is civility, as noted in the previous chapter. If we are to live together in a society, civility is something that we must cherish. In an article for the *Des Moines Register* titled "Classroom Civility Fades Into The Past," a class at Iowa State University is highlighted: The article begins, "The hiss and pop of cans opening can be heard throughout the sweeping banked rows of the Curtiss Hall auditorium. . . . Most settle down when the professor starts to lecture. . . . But in the front row a woman is eating pretzels and drinking a diet Coke. A male student in the back row is reading a science fiction novel. Another woman seems more interested in the student newspaper than the lecture. . . . Students wander in so much as a half-hour late. . . . Others leave fifteen minutes early."[1] Other examples of a loss of civility in our culture can be cited, from road rage to the loss of courtesy in the grocery store. And all this uncivil behavior has dramatically increased due to the pandemic. Again, David Brooks writes, "As Americans' hostility toward one another seems to be growing, their care for one another seems to be falling. A study from Indiana University's Lilly Family School of Philanthropy found that the share of Americans who give to charity is steadily declining. In 2000, 66.2 percent of households made a charitable donation. But by 2018 only 49.6 percent did. The share who gave to religious causes dropped as worship attendance did. But the share of households who gave to secular causes also hit a new low, 42 percent, in 2018."[2] Being charitable and civility go hand in hand.

In an article for the *Baltimore Sun* newspaper, Raymond Burke writes: "The erosion of proper language and social restraint is a symptom of the unwillingness to expect and accept less. It is a reduction in the cost of admission to a place at the table of our approval—a cheapening of our standards. And what plays in the forum of national television soon becomes the copied norm of our everyday discourse."[3] Vulgarity and rude behavior are trampling our civility and contributing to the desensitizing of America.

A third virtue that we are losing is the practice of reverence. Religious leaders are especially aware of this loss. *Webster's Dictionary* defines reverence as "honor or respect felt or shown. . . . Profound, adoring, awed respect." In his book *Reverence: Renewing a Forgotten Virtue*, Paul Woodruff claims that "reverence begins in a deep understanding of human limitations; from this grows the capacity to be awed of whatever we believe lies outside our control—God, truth, justice, nature, and even death."[4]

Living as we do in the most powerful nation on earth, and in an era of such great scientific and technological advancement, it is hard to imagine anything that lies outside our control. Such arrogance is spiritually destructive and has been the death of many civilizations before us. A sense of reverence and awe is a necessary element in the life of the spirit. Woodruff writes, "To forget that you are only human, to think you can act like a god— this is the opposite of reverence. . . . Reverence lies behind civility and all of the graces that make life in society bearable and pleasant. But in our time we hear more praise for irreverence than we do for reverence."

A fourth virtue that needs to be recovered is the ability to reflect. A "headline mentality" is eroding the important place of reflective thought in our lives and actions. Reading the whole story, asking questions, doing research on a given topic, and comparing points of view are all in contrast to the sight, sound, and action world in which we live. We are basically an impatient people who want our food fast, our news in bite-size chunks, and our books in condensed form. There is little patience for any kind of reflective inconvenience that disrupts our surface mentality. And this is becoming increasingly evident within communities of faith.

"Don't just do something, SIT!" is a sign that adorns many Quaker meetinghouses. The activism and dynamism that are so much a part of our civilization can dull our senses and our response to the still, small voice of the Living God. An old cartoon from the *New Yorker* magazine makes an important point. It shows an American couple running up the stairs of the Louvre in Paris, shouting, "Quick, show us the Mona Lisa, we are double-parked!" As with most cartoons, this is funny because it smacks of reality. An erosion of the ability to be reflective is a challenge for religious leaders.

A fifth virtue that has taken a severe hit in recent years is conscience. Many in our society do not seem to have one! A friend of mine told me about a situation that he had experienced at work. A salesman was seeking a 35 percent commission for a sale, but the highest commission that my friend was allowed to give was 25 percent. (It was a sale totaling eight hundred thousand dollars.) When my friend confronted the salesman, the salesman listened politely, and then said, "I know that Christmas is coming up. If you would be willing to approve a 35 percent commission, I will make sure that you receive a nice gift." I am not naive about the ways of the world, but this seems to me a perfect example of the loss of conscience in our society. Multiply this interaction by thousands that occur around our country on a daily basis, and you can see that we have a problem.

For a positive example of conscience, there was a member of a church that I once served, a banker, who was in the process of hiring someone. She shared the following about a reference call she made: "I called on a reference that a teller candidate I was about to hire provided me. The reference told me that he gave the following quotation to our candidate when she was sixteen years old and worked for him at their church. He told her to never forget it. The quotation is this: 'Be governed by principles not by preferences. Compromising values weakens character.' I told her that if she could quote that statement, I would hire her. (I would have hired her anyway, but he told me to ask her to repeat it.) She is now twenty-two years old, and she quoted it word for word." Perhaps there is hope. To refuse to take unethical shortcuts and to honor achievement rather than success, to do something out of principle and to do the right thing rather than the feasible thing, is to participate in the renewal of conscience within ourselves and within our society.

A sixth virtue that needs to be recovered is patience. This is a virtue that our culture is finding in short supply these days: patience at home . . . patience at work . . . patience in all the many relationships that make up who we are . . . and most surely patience in the traffic we confront on the highway. The pandemic has contributed to this lack of patience, but impatience has been with us since the beginning of time. At a certain place in life's journey, patience becomes more and more attractive. The activism of youth rarely understands, nor can it relate to, what it means to try to live life from a patient perspective. In Western culture, "we want it now!" is the mantra by which many live.

My father was a very wise man who grew in wisdom as I matured. One day I came home for lunch following a class during my freshman year in college. He was seated at the kitchen table eating a sandwich and reading a *Christian Century* magazine. In all my impatience and excitement, I told him about a planned protest that I was organizing on campus, over . . . *I forget what.* As I shared with him my youthful enthusiasm for such a protest, he listened and quietly continued to eat his sandwich. Finally, after about a half hour when there was a brief pause in my monologue, he looked up from his reading and said, "Jim, you do not have to die on every cross."

No, *we do not have to die on every cross.* It is only as we grow older that we can begin to gain some perspective and patience as we deal with the issues confronting us. We learn through experience what issues need immediate *impatient* attention and what issues can simmer in *patience.*

Our daughter graduated from Indiana University. She is our only child, so she is a bit spoiled, but very bright. I was never sure, however, until I saw the actual diploma that she was going to make it through college. As smart as she is, she had a difficult time applying her mind to her schoolwork. When given a choice between a party and studying for an exam, she would always choose the party. I spent many a night filled with anxiety worrying about her. When is she going to get serious about life? When, dear God, will her teachable or awakening moment come?

As I have reflected on her high school and college life, I have recognized that my daughter reminds me a lot of myself. If I had a chance to go out with my friends or to a party, the schoolwork would have to wait. It was not until the latter part of my college career that I became serious about my studies and began to have intelligent conversations with my parents. As I proceeded in the academic process, my father would say to me, "I knew you had it in you." I liked hearing that, and I enjoyed making my parents proud.

Sitting in the rain at the football stadium of Indiana University, I looked down at my daughter, one of the thousands graduating, and said to my wife, Elizabeth, "I knew she had it in her." Knowing of my impatience throughout Lisa's growing years and academic life, Elizabeth turned to me with a look that said, "Yeah, right!" I guess that the "I knew she had it in her" was always covered with a few layers of anxiety and impatience.

A friend of mine has a T-shirt that says, "The older I get the wiser I was!" We tend to forget our own foibles, mistakes, and times of impatience. Upon reflection, we were always more poised, more patient, more loving, and more knowledgeable than was the case. Life is like that. We are our own revisionist historians.

Patience . . . It is a virtue that we can use more of these days, and one that religious leaders can help recover by modeling how to be patient with one another.

A *seventh virtue that needs renewal in our society is competence.* Although there is much to decry about today's educational system, we all can carry some of the blame for *incompetency.* Large corporations are offering grants to the American Academy of Arts and Sciences to tell them why their younger middle-level executives cannot write or speak comprehensibly. And we all know the humorous and yet sad examples of college students who think Toronto is in Italy or that Latin class will teach you the language of Latin America. Competence requires the ability to think reflectively and critically on how to deal with the complexities of modern life, as well as to provide persons with a philosophy of life that ethically undergirds all their actions.

An *eighth virtue that we need to recover in our society is the virtue of gratitude.* Gratitude is a practice that is equated with humility, for in expressing gratitude we recognize that we are not alone in this life, and that we are reliant upon God and others for help and support in our daily living and our quest for meaning. Many today have no feelings of humility, nor do they acknowledge their reliance upon others for anything. I believe it was Bart Simpson who, when asked to say grace at the dinner table, said, "Dear God, we paid for all this stuff ourselves, so thanks for nothing!"

The more we mature, we should come to recognize our indebtedness to God, the various communities in which we interact, our families, and our mentors. There is a calming reassurance in acknowledging the truth that we are not in this life experience alone, and that we grow spiritually through our expressions of gratitude for all with whom we come in contact.

One of the things that I like best about living in the Midwest is that most people I meet are ready to converse. I find that a simple trip to the Kroger grocery store can turn into a wonderful time of connecting with others. One of my favorite opportunities to converse is in the checkout line when I swipe my card to pay for what I have purchased, and we all wait for a couple seconds before the machine lights up and says "approved." I love that moment, for it gives me an opportunity to say to the person next to me, as well as the cashier, "Isn't it great to be *approved*." This usually begins a very nice conversation on how important it is to be encouraging to one another and concludes with expressions of gratitude.

I suggest that the two words "thank you" are two of the most significant and powerful words in the English language. And I also believe that gratitude is the most important thing we can express to help us grow spiritually.

A ninth virtue is the virtue of expectant hope. Henri J. M. Nouwen writes, "The first and most basic task of Christian leaders in the future, will be to lead people out of the land of confusion into the land of hope."[5] In this time of transition, people are hungering for hope . . . hope that we will survive this pandemic . . . hope that we will come to our senses and work to stop global warming . . . hope that we will finally come to recognize that as humans we are all connected and in need of one another. From what I have observed, many people are *not* feeling hopeful about the future and have fallen into the trap of negative thinking and cynicism.

Andrew Delbanco is a professor at Columbia University. He wrote a book titled *The Real American Dream: A Meditation on Hope.* In that book, he says what we all know is true, that from time to time in our lives we get the feeling that all the random experiences and sensations and events that we call living do not really add up to anything, that our lives are just meaning-less. The questions are many and are frequently asked by participants in our *Sacred Chaos* seminars: "Why am I here?" "What does life mean?" "What is the purpose of it all?" "Hope," says Delbanco, "is about the stories we tell that help us make meaning out of our lives . . . the stories that restore to us our sense of purpose and worth and make our life worth living again."[6]

The late Peter J. Gomes was the minister at the Memorial Church of Harvard University and the author of numerous books, including *The Scandalous Gospel of Jesus.* In this important book, he writes about hope, and says, "Hope is not the opposite of suffering; suffering is the necessary antecedent of hope because in and through suffering, hope manifests. A hope worth having is forged upon the anvil of adversity. . . . Hope is the stuff that gets us through and beyond when the worst that can happen happens." He continues, "Hope is not merely the optimistic view that somehow everything will turn out all right in the end. . . . Hope is more rugged, the more muscular view that even if things don't turn out all right and aren't all right, we endure through and beyond the times that disappoint or threaten or destroy us."[7]

One of the best examples of expectant hope can be found in the movie *Rudy*. It is one of my favorite movies, primarily because it combines my love of football with my love of the University of Notre Dame. But it is a favorite also because of the expectant hope of the main character. Rudy is the son of a Chicago-area steelworker. He dreams of attending the University of Notre Dame and playing on its football team. Because Rudy is physically too small and mentally too slow, his dream seems completely out of reach. He receives no encouragement from his teachers or coach, and none from his family. In one of the most powerful scenes of the movie, Rudy is seated in the bus station waiting for a ride to South Bend to pursue his dream. His father, quite concerned about his son's mistaken ambition, joins him. Rudy's father tells him the story about a dream his grandfather had of owning a dairy farm in Wisconsin. "He left a good, secure job in the stockyard to chase a crazy dream," he tells his son. "By the end of the first winter, all of the cows had died." End of story. . . . End of dream. And then with a verbal directness designed to burst Rudy's balloon of hope, he says, "You see, Rudy, dreams can destroy you."

Despite the lack of family support, his small size, and his difficulties in learning, Rudy makes the team and graduates from Notre Dame. He probably did not know it at the time and might not now (it is a true story) but Rudy exemplifies the power of the condition of expectant hope . . . the spiritual condition that keeps idealism and dreams alive. And it is in the expectant hope of our dreams and ideals that spiritual growth is made possible.[8]

And then there is the renewal of the virtue of compassion. Renewal of this virtue is perhaps the one that is needed most. With the changing institutional landscape that religious leaders are experiencing, there is the corresponding desensitizing of our society. There is a growing callous disregard for the feelings and welfare of one another. It is a time when children are dying in the custody of our government because their parents are seeking a better life for their families. A Facebook post asks, "If your first response to this news is, 'Were they illegal?' then we don't have a difference in politics, we have a difference in morals." In her writing "Of The Empire," the late poet Mary

Oliver said, "We will be known as a culture that feared death and adored power, that tried to vanquish insecurity for the few and cared little for the many. We will be known as a culture that taught and rewarded the amassing of things, that spoke little if at all about the quality of life for people . . . other people, for dogs, for rivers. All the world, in our eyes, they will say was a commodity. And they will say this structure was held together politically, which it was, and they will say also that our politics was no more than an apparatus to accommodate the feelings of the heart, and that the heart, in those days, was small and hard and full of meanness."[9]

These are not easy words to read, for we are a part of the time that Mary Oliver describes. The loss of compassion for one another is a trajectory on which our society cannot survive. This trajectory is a challenge that religious leaders should feel led to help change.

Most of us live in cocoons, separated from the pain, anguish, hopelessness, and smells of poverty and death that permeate our world. We work hard to maintain our cocoons, from our air-conditioned automobiles passing around such filth on our way to and from work to the changing of channels on our televisions when the news gets too close to our sensibilities. We know how to protect ourselves. And then, on occasion, you hear someone like Mary Cosby, one of the founders of the Church of the Savior in Washington, D.C., share a story of compassion that touches your heart so profoundly that you find yourself weeping. This happened to me when I heard Mary talk about a woman in her church who has a most remarkable job. She is what is called an infant stimulator. She works in a home with physically and mentally challenged children. Her job is to stimulate these children to the degree that they can possibly be stimulated before they die—just to recognize them as human beings. Her name is Abigail. She wrote the following as an assignment for a Christian Testament class. This is the life that she lives among her poor.

"Jamie has olive skin and almond eyes with dark, long lashes. He has thick, beautiful black hair with waves and curls. Jamie is 14 years old and weighs a little over 20 pounds. He has almost no voluntary motion. His little arms and legs contracted, I cradle him on my knee and we play with rattles. His eyes crossed and uncrossed, then focused. His face broke into a smile and then a laugh. We played with rattles a long time, and then he laid his head on my arm. I looked at his beautiful, exquisite Indian face, and felt awe. The mystery of the universe touches me, looks at me, and sees my heart. What awesome being has created this fragile, paper-thin child, and has chosen to inhabit him with his perfect spirit? What awesome fearful being has chosen the total vulnerability of this child, in which to be entrusted in this evil world?

"The evil overwhelms me. The drugs; the cruelty; the lies, and the worship of money and armaments. The sheer cruel hatred that is pouring down the drains and poisoning the ocean of our being. And God so loves the world that God's precious spirit is entrusted to Jamie and is abandoned in a dark and lonely place, waiting to be fed and clothed and bathed and strolled. If no one comes, his little body contracts, and a soft gentle moan comes from this spirit that says, 'I trust; I wait, and I love. Even so, come Lord Jesus.'"

I am always awed, and my heart is always touched, by the compassion shown by such persons as Abigail. When were you last moved to tears by a story or picture of injustice, poverty, or evil in the world? When did such compassion move you to action? How has such compassion changed your life? It is the compassion shown by Abigail that needs to be recovered in today's world.

There is a wonderful story, perhaps apocryphal but nevertheless a great story, about the brilliant scientist and academic Albert Einstein, who was on a train out of New York City. As the conductor came through the passenger coaches, Einstein began to look frantically through his coat pockets for his ticket. By the time the conductor arrived at where Einstein was seated, the great scientist had pulled out all his pockets in both his trousers and coat and was proceeding to search through his briefcase. The conductor, immediately recognizing who Einstein was, said, "Don't worry, Dr. Einstein. I trust you," and proceeded to collect the tickets from the rest of the passengers. After about thirty minutes, the conductor, having finished his ticket collection, was walking back through the car where Einstein was located. By this time, the Princeton professor was blocking the aisle, down on his hands and knees, looking and feeling under the seats and baggage for his ticket. The conductor reiterated, "Dr. Einstein, please don't worry about finding your ticket. I told you that I trust you." To this, Einstein turned his head upward from his position on the floor and said, "Young man, this is not an issue of trust. It is an issue of direction. I have no idea where I am going!"

For religious leaders who are trying to do ministry within a culture that is in chaos, they may be feeling like Einstein: "I have no idea where I am going!" I am convinced that by working on the recovery of certain virtues, we as a culture can find our direction again. Religious leaders not only can help in this recovery, but they also can lead us in this recovery.

The last published words of President Woodrow Wilson, as engraved above his crypt in the Washington National Cathedral in Washington, DC, included this concern: "The sum of the whole matter is this, that our civilization cannot survive materially unless it is redeemed spiritually. It can be saved only by becoming permeated with the Spirit of Christ and made free and happy by the practices which spring out of that spirit." The practices that "spring out of that spirit" at least encompass the ten virtues that are outlined here. May we be courageous enough to reject the current practices of fear, indifference, and insensitivity, and instead seek to concentrate our efforts on recovering the virtues outlined here and, in the words of Woodrow Wilson, *permeate our world with the Spirit of Christ.*

Notes

1. O'Donnell, Thomas R. "Classroom Civility Fades Into The Past." *Des Moines Register*, September 5, 1998.

2. Brooks, David. "America Is Falling Apart at the Seams." *New York Times*, January 13, 2022.

3. Burke, Raymond. *Baltimore Sun*, February 7, 2003.

4. Woodruff, Paul. *Reverence: Renewing a Forgotten Virtue*. Oxford: Oxford University Press, 2014.

5. Nouwen, Henri J. M. *The Wounded Healer: Ministry in Contemporary Society*. New York: Doubleday Image Books, 1972.

6. Delbanco, Andrew. *The Real American Dream: A Meditation on Hope*. Cambridge: Harvard University Press, 1999.

7. Gomes, Peter J. *The Scandalous Gospel of Jesus: What's So Good about the Good News?* San Francisco: HarperOne, 2008.

8. *Rudy*. Released October 13, 1993 by TriStar Pictures, written by Angelo Pizzo and directed by David Anspaugh.

9. Oliver, Mary. "Of The Empire." In *Dream Work*. New York: Grove, 2010.

9

~

Transformation and a
New Spiritual Quest

What does transformation look like? How can religious leaders help and encourage persons who are experiencing transformation? What are the marks of the new spiritual quest that result from transformative experiences?

Christian religious leaders are in the transformation business. We believe that there is a way of life that is much better than the life for which most of us have settled. We believe that Jesus gave us glimpses into this better life and that he modeled for us a way of living that, if emulated, would transform our world. As we make our way through our daily experiences, and as we help others through their experiences, recognizing that all these experiences carry within them the possibility of being "awakening" or "teachable" moments, we become conduits of transformation. The best advice that I have ever been given concerning my own spiritual growth was to pay attention to each moment of life. God is continuously speaking to us, and if we are to grow spiritually, it is up to us to get the message.

The first of my awakening or transformative moments occurred in high school. There was a boy in my class named Junior South. Junior did not fit in with the rest of my class. Because he had been held back at least two grades, he was older than we were. His clothes were tattered, and he spoke in a peculiar Tennessee dialect. Junior entered Burris High School in Muncie, Indiana, in the middle of the eleventh grade and dropped out in the spring. It wasn't a surprise when he did so. After all, he really wasn't one of us. The object of too many bad jokes and the product of a poor home situation, Junior joined the Marines. He desperately needed to find a place where he was accepted and liked for who he was. And he loved his country. This was all I knew about Junior South.

In the fall of my senior year, Junior South was a distant memory. All summer long, my friends and I had been busy with dances and parties, working on our cars, and hanging out at the local Dairy Queen. Of course, there were lawns to mow and odd jobs to do so that we could earn some gas money. For most of the summer, however, we worked harder at playing than we did at working. The Beach Boys modeled a style of life that we sought to emulate. No one ever asked, "Where is Junior?" No one really cared.

I remember sitting in class when the news first began to circulate through the school. "Do you remember Junior South?" *Vaguely.* "He has been killed in Vietnam." It was as though someone had hit me in the stomach. Before this moment, I had never known anyone near my age who had died. Sure, I didn't know him well. I didn't want to know him well. He was different, and he was older, and he talked funny. Now he was dead. Cause of death? The victim of small arms fire.

Junior South did something for me in death that he could not do in life. He made me pay attention to him. A few years ago, while visiting a friend in Washington, D.C., I walked the few short blocks from his office to the Vietnam Veterans Memorial wall, and there I found Junior's name. With the help of a veteran, I traced Junior's name on a sheet of paper, and I wept. I wept for the life of a young man I hardly knew, who I didn't want to know in life, who in death made me pay attention to him. The death of Junior was an *awakening moment* for me, and ever since I have sought to pay attention to all with whom I come in contact, recognizing that even though we may be different, we are all spiritually connected.

Transformative experiences have a way of bursting into our lives from the outside. From outside our socioeconomic group, from outside our "in" group, from outside our ingrown patterns and ways of doing. Have you noticed how in Scripture, it is always the religious insider or the most self-righteous person who is also the most clueless when it comes to a new revelation of God in the world? We experience God in the form of a Samaritan, a leper, a prostitute, or a centurion. Or we experience God in a Junior South, and because of such experiences, we view life from a completely different point of view.

Another transformative experience happened to me on a secluded beach on the coast of North Carolina. My dear friend and mentor had died in December, and my marriage of twenty-five years seemed to be at an end. In an effort to complete two book projects, I was spending the month of February on the coast of North Carolina. The burdens on my heart felt overwhelming, and although I was still functional, I was feeling lonely and depressed. Beginning with the death of my father, life had become a litany of loss. While I was away for this month, my primary motivation to get out of bed in the morning was the anticipation that I would see the sun rise over the beautiful Atlantic Ocean. And so, on this tenth day of my self-imposed exile at the coast, I awakened to the smell of coffee brewing and proceeded to dress into my running suit for what had become my ritual walk to the beach.

The condominium in which I was staying was not more than seventy-five yards from the water. The sun was already casting a pink glow across the horizon, and the ocean waves were rhythmically pounding the shore. It was cold that morning, perhaps in the mid-30s. Everything seemed crisp and alive. I stared off into the vastness of the sea and I began to weep. I lamented where my life on this earth had brought me. Many years of repressed pain flowed up from the pit of my stomach, manifesting in a torrent of tears. Hiding my face behind my cup of hot coffee, I sat down in the sand.

What occurred next is difficult to describe. As clear as if someone were seated next to me, I heard the words, "Everything is going to be all right." I was startled, and I began to glance from side to side, looking for the source of what I had just heard. Again, "Everything is going to be all right." There was no other physical presence on the beach—just me, my cup, and the surf.

I stood up, took my last gulp of coffee, and began to walk the narrow sand-filled path back to my February home. The words, from wherever they had come, brought a strange sense of comfort to my depressing circumstances. "Everything is going to be all right." I was beginning to sense that the chaos through which I had been living had just been tinged with the sacred. The words provided a lining of hope at one of my neediest hours. It was a profoundly spiritual experience, an experience that one feels and which can be understood by only those who have known similar experiences. I believe to this day that the Infinite had reached out to me, a finite man, on a lonely beach in North Carolina, and I have not been the same since.

The spiritual truth that God touches us most profoundly in our vulnerability and pain has a long history within the Christian tradition. One of the most familiar examples comes from the life of Saint Augustine. In his *Confessions*, he tells about his transformation through tears in this way: "So was I speaking and weeping in the most bitter contrition of my heart, when lo! I heard from a neighboring house a voice, as of boy or girl, I know not, chanting and oft repeating, 'Take up and read; take up and read.' Instantly my countenance altered." Augustine interpreted this as a message from God, urging him to pick up his Bible and read. He continues: "I seized, opened, and in silence read that section on which my eyes first fell. 'Not in rioting and drunkenness, not in clambering and wantonness, not in strife and envying; but put ye on the Lord Jesus Christ. . . .' No further would I read; nor needed I: for instantly at the end of this sentence, by a light as it were of serenity infused into my heart, all the darkness of doubt vanished away."[1]

The spiritual quest of Saint Augustine became empowered through the tears of transformation. In like manner, George Fox, the founder of the People called Quakers, heard words that changed his life and the lives of thousands of seekers throughout the world. He had been seeking an authentic faith, a faith that would help answer his numerous questions and give him relief from the depressing circumstances of his life. Finally, he felt that he could seek no further. He felt that he would not find any relief for his hurting soul. And then, he heard a voice that said, "There is one, Christ Jesus, who can speak to thy condition." And then his "heart did leap for joy."[2]

In London, there is a wonderful little pub just off Fleet Street and just down from St. Paul's Cathedral. It is called the Cheshire Cheese. It is here where Samuel Johnson and Charles Dickens would sit for hours keeping their guests and fellow Londoners entranced in conversation. On the front of the menu at the pub, it says, "Newly remodeled." Newly remodeled for the Cheshire Cheese means that it was rebuilt after the Great Fire of London in 1666!

Throughout the Christmas season, I have thought often about my times at the Cheshire Cheese, as we have been treated with Charles Dickens's most famous work in movie version, A Christmas Carol. For those familiar with the work of Dickens, you know that at the heart of much of his thought and writing, there was an empathy for the suffering and oppressed in our world. It was his own experience of childhood poverty and his compassion for people that served as a catalyst for much of his writing.

What is it that makes A Christmas Carol such a popular story and movie? I believe that the primary reason it is such a beloved story is centered in the fact that the main character, Ebenezer Scrooge, was not just educated or comforted by the message of Christmas. No, Ebenezer Scrooge was also transformed by the message of Christmas. Following the visits by the three spirits of Christmas Past, Christmas Present, and Christmas Future, he was radically changed. And such change lasted for not just a day or a week but for the rest of his life.

The most amazing thing about the human personality is that it can be changed, transformed, altered, and redirected. At his grave with the spirit of Christmas Future, Scrooge cries out, "I am not the man I was. I will not be the man I must have been but for these visions. Why show me this if I am past all hope? Good spirit, your nature intercedes for me, and pities me. Assure me that I yet may change these shadows you have shown me by an altered life."

The process of transformation moves through different stages: recognizing that our lives are out of sync with how God would have us live, experiencing the chaos of recognizing such estrangement, and finally being transformed . . . the birth of a new personality. Dickens closes his story about Scrooge by telling us what such transformation looked like for him: "He became as good a friend, as good a master, and as good a man as the good old city knew."[3]

In his book *The Heart of Christianity*, Marcus J. Borg writes about the purpose of spirituality, which he says "is to help birth the new self and nourish the new life." He calls spirituality "midwifery." He writes, "Spirituality is about becoming conscious of and intentional about a deepening relationship with God. . . . What spirituality is about is helping us become aware of a relationship that already exists. In short, spirituality is about the process of being born again, and again, and again."[4]

The Apostle Paul's transformation on the Damascus Road that clearly changed the course of history, the transformations of Saint Augustine and George Fox, and even the transformation of the fictional character Ebenezer Scrooge are all examples of how God enters the human situation, and as a result, the world is changed. William James, the author of the classic book *The Varieties of Religious Experience*, speaks of such experiences as "one of the most remarkable psychological phenomena that is known."[5] As religious leaders, we are called to nurture the transformative experiences of our congregants and encourage the growth in spirit that results. Such experiences of transformation will set those who go through them on new spiritual quests that can move our world in new and positive directions.

It was George Eliot who said during a time similar to the one in which we find ourselves, "We are doing the best that we can through dim lights and tangled circumstances."[6] Every religious leader knows about these *dim lights* and *tangled circumstances*. And yet, even amid the chaos, and perhaps because of the chaos, a new spiritual quest is emerging. Millions of pilgrims who have known transformation have set out on an inward spiritual quest that, they hope, will help define their lives and give their lives new meaning. What these pilgrims hope to find is inner peace amid the conflict and anxiety that fill their lives; a new hope amid the despair that has for too long defined who they are; clarity amid the confusion of media messages; and a passion for life that will sustain them in all they do. The new spiritual quest that is upon us is beginning to brighten the dim lights and untangle the circumstances in which we find ourselves.

At the core of the new spiritual quest is the desire for *a personal relationship with the Living God*. People are hungry to connect with the Infinite, or to know and be known by God, a God who is personal, not remote; who moves us emotionally, not merely intellectually; and whose spirit can be a constant source of strength and stability in a material world that is ever changing. In brief, people want to know God *experientially*.

I was counseling with a woman the other day who has been going through an experience of transition in her faith. She was telling me about how she has felt God working in her experiences and said, "The walls around what I used to believe are crumbling, and I am opening to a new and exciting way of living my faith." Listening to this woman's testimony would give any religious leader a sense of spiritual fulfillment. *Tearing down walls and working with God to open new possibilities for spiritual growth is what we are all about.*

My father would often tell the story about the tourists from Midwestern America who were being guided through Westminster Abbey in London. The guide had spoken for about an hour concerning the architecture and the beauty of the windows, as well as telling about all the historical figures who are buried there. Finally, a woman in the group interrupted the guide saying, "This is all very well, young man, but has anyone been saved here lately?" Although the woman's language may seem archaic to some, she knew how to move from a focus on mere tradition to a focus on what is spiritually significant. For millions of pilgrims today who are experiencing chaos in their lives and in their culture, spiritual significance is centered in a personal relationship with the Living God.

Christian history is filled with reformation and renewal experiences that begin with a movement back to the basics of a personal and direct experience with God. Overemphasis on ritual, heated debate over issues that are not central to the faith, and the cumbersome work of institutional Christianity have all contributed to the inner quest for an experiential spirituality. And such an inner quest will bring about a lifestyle change for those who claim the name "Christian," and for the religious leaders who are responsible for guiding their communities of faith.

Richard Rohr reminds us that "Christianity is a *lifestyle*—a way of being in the world that is simple, non-violent, shared, and loving. However, we made it into an established 'religion' (and all that goes with that) and avoided the lifestyle change itself. One could be warlike, greedy, racist, selfish and vain in most of Christian history, and still believe that Jesus is one's 'personal Lord and Savior.' . . . The world has no time for such silliness anymore. The suffering on Earth is too great."[7]

What are some of the marks of such a lifestyle change that the new spiritual quest envisions?

First, such a lifestyle change will be marked by *a concern for simplicity*. If the ups and downs of a capitalistic culture have taught us anything that is for the good, it is that we need to simplify our lives. The material clutter that has encumbered so many is being replaced with an emphasis on simple living. This emphasis is intensified when one's worldview is expanded.

One does not have to travel very far to realize how the trappings of American wealth keep us insulated from the other three-fourths of the world. A brief plane ride to Haiti or Belize will open one's spiritual eyes to conditions that are difficult to imagine anyone living in. Open sewers, whose stench will never leave you, run throughout Belize City and Port-au-Prince, with children half naked playing along these canals that spread disease and hopelessness. To walk these streets looking into the eyes of the residents, smelling all the different odors that make up such a culture, is to evoke the spiritual yearning for simplification.

A friend of mine makes an annual trip to Haiti during which he works with a group that feeds the hungry. He told me about one of his experiences, when he went with a group that carried two large containers of cooked rice in the back of a truck. As they arrived at this out-of-the-way village, the people came running out of their huts, holding their cupped hands in front of them, begging for the rice. Within ten minutes, all the rice was devoured by the hungry villagers.

This kind of life is unimaginable for most of us who live in well-fed America. As a result of his frequent trips to Haiti, my friend is constantly in search of ways he can simplify his own life. He has learned what is spiritually important.

Another mark of this new spiritual quest and lifestyle change is *the quest for diversity and inclusivity*. One cannot have an authentic, transformational experience with the Living God and simplify one's life so that spiritual growth is given priority, and not have it issue a concern for diversity and inclusivity.

Along with millions of others on New Year's Eve, I watched CNN with Anderson Cooper and Andy Cohen as they reported on the huge party in Times Square. As the crystal ball dropped at exactly midnight, and as "New York, New York" played in the background, the camera focused on persons in the crowd. There were Asians, African Americans, gay, straight, and transgender, White and Hispanic people, all embracing and all loving one another. As CNN ended its coverage, Anderson Cooper, a gay man himself, shared a message of hope as he commented about the acceptance of openly gay reporters covering New Year celebrations around the world.

The new spiritual quest includes a quest for diversity and inclusivity as we grow in love and understanding of one another.

Recently a friend sent me the following from Michael Gerson, which I now keep on my desk as a reminder of what the image of God in our midst should look like: "What if every man and every woman—every victim of abuse, every abandoned child, every lonely senior, every intellectually and physically challenged person, every single person, every gay, transgender person, every prisoner, every homeless person, everyone we love and everyone we fear, were actually the image of God in our midst, equal in humanity, in dignity and worth. *How should we then live?*"[8] (italics added). A wonderful query for each of us to consider.

Another mark of this new lifestyle change is *a concern for peace*. As I write, Russia is invading Ukraine. The bloody and violent images coming out of Ukraine are sickening. Where this will lead we do not know, but it is clear that there will be many lives lost and great disruption to a country that has been trying to live in peace. "Blessed are the peacemakers," says Jesus in his Sermon on the Mount. America has known war and violence since its inception, as have Russia and Ukraine, with little respite between conflicts. The concern for peace is no longer something that can be relegated to just the "traditional" peace churches . . . Mennonites, Brethren, and Quakers. In today's world, it needs to be a concern for all Christians and their leadership.

The authors of this book are both Quakers by tradition who have sought to live according to the Quaker *Peace Testimony*. From the beginning of the Quaker movement in the mid-seventeenth century, Quakers have tried to be peacemakers and live in that *light and love* that take away the occasion for war and violence. Many have called Quakers impractical. Conversely, I suggest that war and violence are not practical, and in the words of William Penn, "It is time to see what love can do."

In 1661, the early Quakers sent a declaration to King Charles II. It read, in part,

> We utterly deny all outward wars and strife and fightings with outward weapons, for any end or under any pretense whatsoever. And this is our testimony to the whole world. The Spirit of Christ, by which we are guided, is not changeable, so as once to command us from a thing as evil and again to move unto it; and we do certainly know, and so testify to the world, that the Spirit of Christ, which leads us into all Truth, will never move us to fight and war against any person with outward weapons, neither for the kingdom of Christ, nor for the kingdoms of this world.

One person whom most people revere as an example of a life lived with God is Mother Teresa. In her "Reflections on Working Toward Peace," Mother Teresa shares these important words:

> The fruit of silence is prayer; the fruit of prayer is faith; the fruit of love is service; the fruit of service is peace. Let us not use bombs and guns to overcome the world. Let us use love and compassion. Let us radiate the peace of God and so light His light and extinguish in the world and in the hearts of all people all hatred and love for power. Today if we have no peace, it is because we have forgotten that we belong to each other. That man, that woman, that child is my brother or sister. If everyone could see the image of God in his or her neighbor, do you think we would still need tanks and generals?

She continues: "Peace begins at home. If we truly want peace in the world, let us begin by loving one another in our own families."[9] Perhaps this is too simple or, as the Quakers have been called, *impractical.* I am convinced, however, that the path to peace on the streets of American cities and in the world begins with such small, simple steps. It is tempting to tell ourselves that we cannot make a difference in this world of violence, to throw up our arms and say, "This is as good as it gets." This rationalization, however, should not prevent us from *trying* to live a life of radical love and from sharing this love with as many of our fellow travelers in this life as we can. This, I believe, is what Jesus envisioned.

The quest for justice is another mark of a transformed lifestyle. As one grows spiritually, certain inner changes begin to happen. War will become abhorrent. The physical and spiritual hunger of the poor and destitute will make your own heart ache. What is happening in poor and war-torn countries around the world will haunt your thoughts in the day and your dreams at night. Each time a cruelty is done to another, each time someone is put down, called names, or bullied to increase the worldly favor of another, your own being will cry out in empathy. To grow spiritually is to see the world and humanity as God sees the world and humanity.

The ways of the world encourage individualism, but growth in the spirit of Christ will accentuate the interconnectedness of all people and the care we should have for one another.

I am reminded of the words of John Donne, who wrote, "No man is an island, entire of itself; every man is a piece of the continent, a part of the main. If a clod be washed away by the sea, Europe is the less. . . . Any man's death diminishes me, because I am involved in mankind; and therefore, never send to know for whom the bell tolls; it tolls for thee."[10] The point that

Donne wants us to understand is that on this great big blue marble that we call Earth, *we belong to one another*. Don't ask "who has died?" when you hear the bells in the churchyard; *it tolls for thee*. Whenever someone dies, a bit of you has died as well. We are all connected. . . . We are all intertwined. . . . In the new spiritual quest, this connection becomes apparent, and a concern of justice *for me* is a concern of justice *for us all*, recognizing that as individuals we cannot be separated from our fellow human beings.

Each of us will experience God in different ways. Transforming moments come to our souls through various avenues. Most of us will not have the same transformative experiences that the Apostle Paul, Saint Augustine, George Fox, or the fictional character Ebenezer Scrooge experienced. By paying attention to our life experiences, however, we can prepare for the possibility of new and transformative *awakening moments*. These moments give the journey of life meaning, which will issue in a new spiritual quest marked by a movement toward *simplicity*, toward *diversity and inclusivity*, toward *peace and justice*. To live in the expectant rhythm of such transformational moments is to learn the secret of living in the fullest sense.

Notes

1. Augustine. *The Confessions of Saint Augustine*. Translated by Sarah Ruden. New York: Modern Library, 1949.

2. Fox, George. *The Journal of George Fox*. Edited by John Nickalls. Philadelphia: Philadelphia Yearly Meeting, 1997.

3. Dickens, Charles. *A Christmas Carol*. London: Chapman and Hall, 1843.

4. Borg, Marcus J. *The Heart of Christianity: Rediscovering a Life of Faith*. San Francisco: HarperCollins, 2003.

5. James, William. *The Varieties of Religious Experience: A Study in Human Nature*. New York: Modern Library, 1902.

6. Eliot, George. *Middlemarch*. Kolkata: Signet Press, 2004. (First published in 1871.)

7. Rohr, Richard. Facebook page, February 17, 2022. www.facebook.com/David Wheeler.

8. Gerson, Michael. "Faith Requires Us to Be Outraged at Every Violation of Human Dignity." *Deseret*, May 10, 2018. https://www.deseret.com/2018/5/10/20644838/faith-requires-us-to-be-outraged-at-every-violation-of-human-dignity.

9. Mother Teresa. "Reflections on Working Toward Peace." *Architects of Peace*. Santa Clara: Santa Clara University.

10. Donne, John. *Devotions, Meditation 17*. Cambridge: The University Press, 1923.

10

Authentic Religious Leadership and Digging a New Well

Are you able to be authentic and real with your congregation? How are you build-ing trust with congregants? As a religious leader, are you prepared to dig a new well in a world that is spiritually thirsty?

Like many of you, I watched the PBS series *Country Music* produced by historian Ken Burns. I have never been much of a country music fan, but this program really grabbed my attention. I found the tragedies associated with many of the country music musicians quite moving. The alcohol and drug abuse of Hank Williams, and his death at the young age of twenty-nine. The tragic plane crash that took the life of Patsy Cline at the age of thirty. The alcohol addiction of George Jones and the difficult life of Loretta Lynn all were put on full display during Ken Burns's documentary.

I have been trying to understand what is so attractive about country music, and the one word that keeps coming back to me is "authenticity." Whatever else country music is, it is *authentic*. It speaks about the real-life issues that many people face in their everyday lives. Beyond the twangy gui-tars and the yodeling, there is a message that touches people where they live. Many of the songs have touched my heart as well.

Authenticity. . . . It is a word that has become more and more meaningful to me in recent years. I find myself tired of people who lack authenticity, who are living lives based in delusion or on lies . . . persons who are constantly gaming the system, and who are in this world for only themselves . . . persons who live by talking points and who are dishonest with themselves and oth-ers. For religious leaders, *authenticity*, or being *real*, should be at the center of who they are and what they represent as ministers in the new world that is being born.

Over the years, I have found many important truths in books that were written primarily for children. At this particular time in my life, I am especially fond of the children's book *The Velveteen Rabbit*. Within the pages of this beautiful book, a conversation about what is *real* is recorded between the Skin Horse and the Rabbit:

> "What is real?" asked the Rabbit one day. "Does it mean having things that buzz inside of you and a stick-out handle?" "Real isn't about how you are made," said the Skin Horse. "It's a thing that happens to you. When a child loves you for a long, long time, not just to play with, but really loves you, then you become real."
>
> "Does it hurt?" inquired the Rabbit. "Sometimes," said the Skin Horse, for he was always truthful. "When you are real you don't mind being hurt." The Rabbit continues his questioning: "Does it happen all at once, like being wound up, or bit by bit?"
>
> "It doesn't happen all at once," responded the Skin Horse, "You become. It takes a long time. That is why it doesn't often happen to people who break easily, or who have sharp edges, or who have to be carefully kept. Generally, by the time you are real, most of your hair has been loved off, and your eyes drop out and you get loose in the joints and very shabby. But these things don't matter at all, because once you are real you can't be ugly, except to people who don't understand."[1]

Within today's faith community, people are looking for religious leaders who are *real* and who are *authentic*. No one wants to be in relationship with persons who are *not* real and who are phony and pretentious. To be real means that we are honest with one another, and open with one another about our failings and successes. In short, the religious leader of today is one who can share his or her sorrows without fear and celebrate his or her joys openly.

While I was going through a divorce, I received a call from a former student. He was angry that I was divorcing and claimed that I had failed him and others who looked up to me. I let him speak for a while, and then at the end of his scolding, I said, "You know, Bob, staying on that pedestal where you placed me took way too much of my spiritual and emotional energy. I'm sorry to be such a disappointment to you." Upon reflection, what my wife and I were experiencing together throughout our divorce (we eventually remarried) was the growth process described by the Skin Horse to the Rabbit. We were becoming real with one another. For my wife and me, it was radical relationship surgery, and we would not change what we both went through for the new relationship that we are experiencing.

An important part of being real and authentic is not hiding behind the mystique of infallibility. Congregations (and students) tend to put their religious leaders on a pedestal. Many want to believe that they can do no wrong. We are *not* infallible, and we *can* do wrong. Like everyone else, religious leaders need to constantly ask for forgiveness for human failings, and trust that our belief in a God of new beginnings will forgive us and give us a new beginning. And the good news is that of these new beginnings there is no end.

Religious leaders who are real, authentic, and fallible will gain the trust of their congregants. And trust of leadership will be needed for the hard task of institutional transformation that lies before us in the new spiritual landscape that is continuously forming. The new religious leader for our time will be one who understands the transitional time we are in and the need to dig a new well.

In his book *Sacred Eyes*, L. Robert Keck writes, "If an old institution is to tap into the new soul-river, it must be courageous enough to dig a new well. If religious institutions are not up to that transformative task, they will eventually fail to serve as a re-connecting force for their people, will lose legitimacy, and will eventually die."[2]

These words make all of us associated with religious institutions uncomfortable. As the previous chapters of this volume have indicated, "transition" is the normative word for our day. It is hard to dig a new well, but dig new wells we must.

The purpose of a religious institution should not be mere survival alone. Jesus did not live and die because the world in which he lived, to quote a Jack Nicholson movie title, was *as good as it gets*. No, Jesus envisioned a *new* world and a *new* way of living. *Jesus dug a new well.* Many of our institutions that have long since lost their vitality and reason for existence are still surviving. All that it takes is some endowment funds, a strong tradition, and a religious leader comfortable in maintaining the status quo. Most of our institutions, however, are working to *thrive*, not merely survive. If the religious institutions that we serve are to thrive in a new, transformative world, the focus question is "How do we equip our congregations to reach out to a spiritually hungry world more effectively?" *Not* "How do we keep our congregants content by maintaining the status quo?"

The spiritual hunger in the world today can be simply stated by a question that Karl Barth famously asked. "Is it true?" he writes. "This talk of a loving and good God, who is more than one of the friendly idols whose rise is so easy to account for, and whose dominion is so brief? What the people want to find out and thoroughly understand is, 'Is it true?' . . . They want to find out and thoroughly understand the answer to this *one question*, and not some answer that beats about the bush."[3] Every religious leader I know wants it to be true, and most are conscientious and sincere in their search to discover if it is true. There are also times, however, when during this search even the most devout leaders have doubts. Doubts lead to questions, and questions tend to lead to more questions. Asking questions, however, is not something to stifle one's growth in spirit; questions enhance our growth. If religious leaders have earned the respect and trust of their congregations, the leaders will be able to bring their congregants on the journey of search with them. As already noted in the preceding chapters, sometimes this search will be difficult and chaotic, and it can stretch the boundaries of comfort wherein many congregations like to reside. But if the twenty-first-century search for a response to "Is it true?" is conducted lovingly and with the clear intent to grow spiritually, it can be transformational, both for religious leaders and for their congregations.

There are at least four marks that are part of a searching and thriving congregation, a congregation that is digging a new well and whose members are on a spiritual quest to respond to the question "Is it true?"

The first mark is *transformational experience*. I have written about this experience in previous chapters, and I see this experience as an essential part of the new well. I was a young boy when I first heard the words of the seventeenth-century theologian Robert Barclay. Sitting in the silence of Minneapolis Friends Meeting, I heard my father repeat the following words many times as he spoke out of the silence: "For when I came into the silent assemblies of God's people, I felt a secret power among them, which touched my heart, and as I gave way unto it I found the evil weakening in me and the good raised up."

The transforming power of Barclay's testimony can still touch my heart. A searching and thriving congregation seeks to be a place where people can congregate and experience the evil weakening within them and feel the good being raised up. Such transformation can be one of immediacy, like Barclay's, or one that is experienced in increments, as Malcolm Muggeridge would describe his transformation. Here is what Muggeridge wrote in his book *A Twentieth Century Testimony*:

> When I look back on my life nowadays, which I sometimes do, what strikes me most forcibly about it is that what seemed at the time most significant and seductive, seems now most futile and absurd. For instance, success in all of its various guises: being known and being praised; ostensible pleasures, like acquiring money or seducing women, or traveling, going to and fro in the

world and up and down in it like Satan, exploring and experiencing whatever vanity fair has to offer.

In retrospect all these exercises in self-gratification seem pure fantasy, what Pascal called 'licking the earth.' They are diversions designed to distract our attention from the true purpose of our existence in the world, which is, quite simply, to look for God, and in looking, to find God, and having found God, to love God, thereby establishing a harmonious relationship with God's purposes for God's creation.[4]

At the heart of a religious leader's task in the digging of this new well is helping his or her congregation to develop a *density of readiness* for the kind of spiritually transformative experience to which Robert Barclay and Malcolm Muggeridge testified. The deadening crust of tradition and emphasis upon correct process and procedure need to give way to the fresh winds of God's transforming spirit. The sacred cows of the past need to be examined to see if they help or hinder the search for a response to "Is it true?" In my time as a church consultant, I often asked congregations, "How many small spiritual nurture and prayer groups are a part of your congregation?" I have found that churches that have many small groups that are gathering for prayer and for spiritual learning and renewal are more likely to be open to the kind of transformation needed to dig a new well.

A second mark of a searching and thriving congregation is its ability to *nurture community*. This has been an important emphasis that has been outlined in previous chapters. I love Parker Palmer's definition of community. He says, "Community is that place where the person you least want to be with is always present. And the addendum to this truth is, when that person leaves or dies, there is always someone else to take his or her place!" Being in community can be difficult. Persons are not easy to deal with. They are stubborn . . . they say stupid things . . . they don't like me . . . I don't like them. And yet we are asked by our Lord to forgive one another . . . to love one another . . . to care for one another and to encourage one another.

The new well being dug needs a nurturing community to model a way of life that is loving and caring toward one another. This nurturing community needs to illustrate to the world that such a community is possible. In his book *The God of Jesus*, Stephen J. Patterson writes about the kind of community that Jesus envisioned. He writes,

Jesus believed that the experience of God he had could be translated into human relationships and forms of community. That is why he began to speak about a new Empire of God. To speak about a new Empire, a reign, is to speak about life in its greatest corporate aspect, life together. How did he imagine this?

Picture a table, It is large and lavished with foods of every sort and drink. Around it are gathered the children of God. They are not your peers. They are brought here by another invitation. Each has been drawn to the table by the inviting power of God's love. They have come as they are, some in rags, some in rich finery, some washed, some not, some are alone, some sit as families, some speak your language, most do not. There is a man you know, who has utterly destroyed his life and that of those around him that he seems beyond redemption. He waits. There is a woman whose shoulders curl high. She sits at the head of the table. There is a young child, thin and drawn, with hollow cheeks but eager eyes. She has already begun to eat. A beggar slips into a chair, unsure of his place but willing to risk it. He tries to blend in. And so it goes around this infinite expanse of table, containing practical things: food, company, belonging, care, honor—the necessities of life. Here they are offered to each; all have access to what is needed. This is the communal form of love.

Patterson continues, "Jesus' vision for what human community might be like came from his experience of God. If God is that fundamental reality running through all of life and existence, and if the character of that reality is love, then the finest, most authentic form of human community must in some way embody love."[5]

A searching and thriving congregation knows how to nurture community and to share with the world the kind of love for one another that Jesus envisioned. Any form of a new well will need to be a place where this kind of community is taken seriously.

A third mark of such a congregation is the *cultivation of conviction.* A part of the purpose of any thriving, beloved community is helping people of the "Is it true?" search to know *what* they believe and *why* they believe it. For many years, I was part of an effort to explore ways that each local congregation could become a seminary . . . *a theological school for all members.* The center of practical theological discourse where the "why" questions can be asked is the congregation. Although the teaching office of the Church has many different foci, e.g., the seminary, continuing education centers, ecumenical organizations, church-related colleges, etc., the local congregation is the one place that seeks to ground theological discourse in the practical life experiences of everyday Christians. These believers, who are living their lives as best they know how with the help of genuine faith commitments, need the congregation to be that place of inquiry into theological issues that are forever being raised in their practical experiences of life. "I believe in God, but my child has just been killed. How can I make sense of my belief in a loving God since this happened?" "I prayed all night that my mother would be healed of her illness, and it didn't work. How do I pray correctly for healing?" "My husband has left me. He says that he no longer loves me. The Bible says that I should not get a divorce except in the case of adultery. What should I do?" "I work in an armaments factory. I feel guilty making weapons of destruction, but I am the sole breadwinner for my family. How do I discern God's will for my life and vocation?" All of these represent practical theological questions. It is in the life experiences of church members that theology moves from the abstract to the practical, and the congregational setting is where these practical issues can be reflected upon.

On the whole, the teaching task of the Church has been sorely neglected in many congregations. What passes for Bible study in numerous places is just a time of fellowship when trite phrases are repeated and one's religious prejudices are recited. A most important task of religious leaders who are digging a new well is to help their congregants *become self-reflective and think critically.* So many ministers will graduate from seminary and immediately forget all that they learned about the critical study of Scripture or how to help persons reflect on who they are and why they are here. Religious leaders can easily be overwhelmed with the administrative tasks of the church and the daily crises in the congregation that are forever thrust upon them, and the spiritual tasks of self-reflection and critical thinking can easily be neglected.

Recently I was home sick, lying in bed with a cold washcloth on my head, trying to bring down a fever. I had been up most of the night, and I was filled with medicine. To say the least, I was not feeling well. I made the mistake of having the television on, listening to some talk show. On this particular day, the topic was about God. The question was, "Does God exist?" The show's producer had arranged to have a brilliant atheist philosopher argue against God's existence. She was very good and made some compelling arguments. On the other side of the issue was some evangelical television preacher. He could not give one compelling reason for the existence of God and spoke in trite, "you just have to have faith"-type phrases. I lay there, sick and getting sicker, wondering to myself, "Is this the best spokesperson the media could find to discuss such an important topic?" For me, as a professing Christian, it was embarrassing and humiliating, and just listening to this discussion made my fever go up!

In her Gifford lectures *The Life of the Mind,* Hannah Arendt states that her interest in "mental activities" had many sources but was most immediately influenced by the Eichmann trial in Jerusalem. In observing Adolf Eichmann respond to questions, she wrote that he showed no evidence of being able to "stop and think," but rather spoke in "cliche-ridden language."[6]

To "stop and think" and to examine our actions in a reflective way as we interact within our various worlds of activity are becoming less and less part of our lives. "Cliche-ridden" language abounds, and although we may not experience the demonic ways of the Nazi Eichmann, we know something about the thoughtlessness of his existence. Thoughtlessness is everywhere in today's world, the by-products being minds without rudders floating in a sea of confusion. And for many millions, religion, in the traditional sense, has failed to provide the necessary certainty to clarify the confusion.

Humans need to perceive meaning in life. In this human search for meaning, there is value in psychological and sociological reflection, for these disciplines inform our search. But they do not get at the core issue of the search and ask the questions "Why am I here?" and "Is it true?" These questions cannot be discovered in the writings of Carl Jung or Max Weber, though they are helpful. To begin the pursuit of asking such reflective questions, we need to begin within the realm of *theology*.

If we are digging a new well, an important part of a religious leader's ministry is helping his or her congregants to think critically and reflectively, and this most certainly means using these tools in any philosophical endeavor as well as on Scripture. Searching and thriving congregations are serious about the religious-education task of the church, and they are developing classes that *not only inform the mind but also awaken the heart*.

A fourth mark of a searching and thriving congregation is its *vision toward ministry and service*. When a congregation is focused inward on the question "How do we keep our members content?" it has missed its call. A new and bold ministry and service thrust should be an important part of any new well that is dug. When religious leaders and the congregations they serve focus outward on meeting the needs of a hurting world, they surrender themselves to something outside of themselves, and new life is the result. "What are the needs of the community in which we reside?" "Who is hurting and needs a helping hand?" "How can we meet these needs and heal these hurts?"

Religious leaders and religious institutions are in the midst of a whirlwind of chaos and change. History shows that out of every chaotic period in the past, new ideas, new directions, and new life have formed and developed. Religious institutions have prevailed through the darkest of times and have historically been like anvils wearing out many cultural hammers. They can be, at their best and even now, one of the prisms through which the Divine Light passes. And religious leaders, *if* they can be nurtured and encouraged to be authentic and real in this time of chaos as well as in the chaos of their personal lives, *can* emerge with *awakened hearts* and a *prophetic voice*. The digging of the new well needs leadership, and the spiritual journey of asking "Is it true?" is forever unfolding.

Notes

1. Bianco, Margery Williams. *The Velveteen Rabbit*. Garden City: Doubleday, 1982.

2. Keck, L. Robert. *Sacred Eyes*. Synergy Associates, 1993.

3. Barth, Karl. *The Word of God and the Word of Man*. Gloucester: Peter Smith Publishers, 1958.

4. Muggeridge, Malcolm. *A Twentieth Century Testimony*. Nashville: Thomas Nelson, 1978.

5. Patterson, Stephen J. *The God of Jesus: The Historical Jesus and the Search for Meaning*. Harrisburg: Trinity Press International, 1998.

6. Arendt, Hannah. *Thinking*. The Life of the Mind, vol. 1. New York: Harcourt, Brace and Jovanovich, 1971.

~

Epilogue

A Model of Spirituality in a Time
of Tribalism and Chaos

Get the writings of John Woolman by heart.

—Charles Lamb

As repeatedly noted throughout this volume, we are living in a divisive time. One *New York Times* reporter called this a time of *tribalism*. Rich versus poor, North versus South, White versus Brown and Black, well educated versus poorly educated, and so forth. However defined, it is uncomfortable, and it is tearing at the fragile fabric that holds us together as a society and as communities of faith. Such tribalism has been a major contributor to the chaos that we are all feeling.

As we search for a calming spiritual presence in today's world of anxiety-raisers, we are helped by the signposts left us by the spiritual giants of the past. And no one is a more calming and yet prophetic spiritual influence than John Woolman. Few writings have meant more to me over the years than *The Journal of John Woolman*. In this *Journal*, Woolman tells about his life, travels, and ever-deepening social conscience. It was the former president of Harvard University Charles Lamb who said of Woolman in his introduction to volume one of the "Harvard five-foot shelf," "Get the writings of John Woolman by heart." "By heart" is really the only way to "get" the writings of Woolman. They defy the world's traditional reason.

John Woolman's faith was one of *profound simplicity*. He struggled long and hard with the difficult issues associated with the faith by which he sought to live. Early in his life, he was confused about his relationship with God, living, as he called it, from "one youthful vanity to another." As he matured spiritually, however, and after he dealt with his own chaos and confusion,

135

he was able to work through the more cumbersome issues surrounding his beliefs, and by remaining close to what he called "inner promptings," he was able to live in a close yet simple relationship with God.

In many ways, Woolman reminds me of Mother Teresa. Her good friend Malcolm Muggeridge once shared with me the story of a time when Mother Teresa was invited to be on a television program with a panel of Christian leaders discussing their faith. Here were the archbishop of Canterbury and other world-renowned theologians. And then there was Mother Teresa. When asked to explain her faith following the very eloquent dissertations of the other guests, who could be very impressive academically, Mother Teresa said, "Oh, I try to follow the example of Jesus. I just want to love as Jesus would have me love . . . care for the sick, feed the hungry, and love the poor."

Following the program, the archbishop was heard to say, "You know, if I had to spend much time with that woman, I would be in real trouble!" The "trouble" that this simplicity of faith causes is that when we are in the presence of such powerful examples of Christlikeness as Woolman or Mother Teresa, we experience the discomfort of knowing how far we are from such a spirituality. It is a childlike openness to the working of the Living God. It is not a simplistic faith but a faith of profound simplicity.

There is a certain passage in the *Journal* that has always moved me deeply. It has to do with Woolman's description of his own transformation. It begins with these words:

> While I silently ponder on that change wrought in me, I find no language equal to it nor any means to convey to another a clear idea of it. I looked upon the works of God in this visible creation and an awfulness covered me; *my heart was tender and often contrite, and a universal love to my fellow creatures increased in me.* This will be understood by such who have trodden in the same path. Some glances of real beauty may be seen in their faces who dwell in true meekness. There is a harmony in the sound of that voice to which divine love gives utterance. . . . Yet all these do not fully show forth that inward life to such who have felt it. (italics added)

In this statement, Woolman succinctly captures the meaning of *spiritual transformation*. Transformation is expressed in the *tenderizing of one's heart* and issues in an increase of *universal love to one's fellow creatures*. What does having one's heart grow tender mean? What are the marks of such a process? How do I begin to experience, and how can our society experience, that sense of awe that finds expression in a tender and contrite heart?

A profound sense of spiritual humility is the first mark of a tender heart. Those persons with tender hearts do not boast or intimidate. They are not braggarts or bullies. The tenderhearted are not self-righteous or judgmental. They do not insist on their own way, espousing certitudes that love and reflective thought have not tested. Humility has been a part of the lives of all who seek to grow in spirit and is an important signpost given us by those who have traveled the path of spiritual growth. John Woolman possessed a humility born of a tender heart.

Another mark of a heart growing in love toward God and one another, and which is beautifully illustrated in the life of John Woolman, is *a sense of connection with human suffering.* Within the Christian tradition, a tender heart is a heart that is broken by what breaks the heart of Jesus.

John Woolman felt this connection with suffering in a profound way. In his *Journal,* he records a dream in which he saw a mass of matter to the south and to the east. As he reflected upon this dream, he became aware that this mass was human beings in great misery (African American slaves). The misery was so great that Woolman could hear their crying and their wails of pain. As he struggled to interpret this dream, Woolman was suddenly enlightened with the insight that he was "mixed with" these people who were suffering. Their cries of pain were his cries of pain. They were spiritually connected. This connection became a lifelong ministry as Woolman spoke out against slavery. Alfred North Whitehead said that Woolman stood at that pivotal point in human history when we began to envision a civilization without slavery. It is said that Woolman's protests against slavery were so effective among his fellow Quakers that sixty years before that famous first shot at Fort Sumter that began the Civil War, no Quaker was known to have owned a slave. A sense of connection with human suffering is a characteristic of a tender heart.

Woolman's tender heart was demonstrated also in his *caring and sensitivity toward the entire created order.* A love of all of God's creation is a component of a tender heart. Woolman's heart would break if he were to see pictures of big-game hunters posing by the corpses of lions, tigers, and elephants that these hunters had shot dead. In his day, he had a sensitivity shown in his concern for the way animals were treated, particularly the way horses were treated by carriage drivers. Toward the end of his life when he traveled to England, Woolman refused to ride in carriages because the drivers ran their horses to death to meet schedules that were too tight. Instead, Woolman walked everywhere. A tender heart cares for the entire created order.

John Woolman lived a life of simplicity and worked tirelessly for peace in our diverse world. He lived a life of integrity, and he loved his faith community. Woolman worked his entire life on issues of equality, and he felt a sense of stewardship for all of God's creation. If there ever were a need for the spirituality that John Woolman lived, it is now. He is indeed a model of spirituality in a time of tribalism and chaos.

In his pamphlet "A Plea for the Poor," John Woolman wrote from his tender heart and his increasing love for all. It seems a fitting conclusion to a book designed to help religious leaders who find themselves in sacred chaos as well as who find themselves trying to define the perils and promise of the new world of ministry that is opening to them. Woolman is brief and succinct:

> Our gracious Creator cares and provides for all his Creatures. His tender mercies are over all his works; and so far as his love influences our minds, so far as we become interested in his workmanship, and feel a desire to take hold of every opportunity to lessen the distresses of the afflicted and increase the happiness of the Creation. Here we have a prospect of one common interest, from which our own is inseparable, that to turn all of the treasures that we possess into the channel of Universal Love, becomes the business of our lives.[1]

Amid uncertainty and pain, social rifts, tribalism, and misinformation, we encounter the words of Julian of Norwich. . . .

And all shall be well . . .
And all shall be well . . .
And all manner of things shall be well . . .

Note

1. Woolman, John. *The Journal and Major Essays of John Woolman*. Edited by Amelia Gummere. New York: Macmillan, 1992.

~

Bibliography

"7 Examples of Self-Awareness in Everyday Life." April 21, 2020, by Kara McD. https://myquestionlife.com/examples-of-self-awareness-in-everyday-life/.

Allen, Mike. "QAnon infects churches." *Axios*, May 31, 2021. https://www.axios.com/2021/05/31/qanon-churches-popular-religion-conspiracy-theory.

Arendt, Hannah. *Thinking*. The Life of the Mind, vol. 1. New York: Harcourt, Brace and Jovanovich, 1971–77.

Augustine. *The Confessions of Saint Augustine*. New York: Modern Library, 1949.

Bailie, Gil. *Violence Unveiled: Humanity at the Crossroads*. Pearl River: Crossroad Publishing Company, 1995.

Baker, Adam. Facebook page, January 22, 2022. www.facebook.com/Adam Baker.

Barna Group. Ventura, California.

Barth, Karl. *The Word of God and the Word of Man*. Gloucester: Peter Smith Publishers, 1958.

Beattie, Melody. *Journey to the Heart: Daily Meditations on the Path to Freeing Your Soul*. San Francisco: HarperSanFrancisco, 1996.

Beattie, Melody. *The Language of Letting Go: Daily Meditations on Codependency*. San Francisco: HarperCollins, 1990.

Bianco, Margery Williams. *The Velveteen Rabbit*. Garden City: Doubleday, 1982.

Borg, Marcus J. *The Heart of Christianity: Rediscovering a Life of Faith*. San Francisco: HarperCollins, 2003.

Boyle, Gregory. *Tattoos on the Heart: The Power of Boundless Compassion*. New York: Simon and Schuster, 2010.

Britain Yearly Meeting. *Quaker Faith and Practice*. Warwick: Warwick Printing Company, 1995.

Brogdon, Lewis. "The Fight for the Soul of America." *Christian Ethics Today*, Summer 2021.

Brooks, David. "America Is Falling Apart at the Seams." *New York Times*, January 13, 2022.

Buechner, Frederick. *The Sacred Journey: A Memoir of Early Days.* New York: HarperCollins, 1982.

Burke, Raymond. *Baltimore Sun,* February 7, 2003.

Cahill, Thomas. *How the Irish Saved Civilization: The Untold Story of Ireland's Heroic Role from the Fall of Rome to the Rise of Medieval Europe.* New York: Anchor Books, 1995.

Camus, Albert. *The Plague.* New York: Vintage Books, 1975.

"Classroom Civility Fades Into The Past." *Des Moines Register,* September 5, 1998. www.contemplativemonk.com.

Deavel, David P. and Wilson, Jessica Hooten. *Solzhenitsyn and American Culture: The Russian Soul in the West.* South Bend: University of Notre Dame Press, 2020.

Delbanco, Andrew. *The Real American Dream: A Meditation on Hope.* Cambridge: Harvard University Press, 1999.

Dickens, Charles. *A Christmas Carol.* London: Chapman and Hall, 1843.

Donne, John. *Devotions, Meditation 17.* Cambridge: The University Press, 1923.

Eliot, George. *Middlemarch.* Kolkata: Signet Press, 2004. (First published in 1871.)

EquaSion. "A *Mighty Stream* Discussion Guide on Race and Racial Equity." 2022. *Facebook.* <www.facebook.com>.

Florer-Bixler, Melissa. "Why Pastors Are Joining the Great Resignation." *Sojourners,* November 30, 2021.

Fournier, Ron and Sophie Quinton. "In Nothing We Trust." *The Atlantic,* April 12, 2012.

Frost, Robert. "Mending Wall." *North of Boston.* London: David Nutt, 1914.

Fox, George. *The Journal of George Fox.* Edited by John Nickalls. Philadelphia: Philadelphia Yearly Meeting, 1997.

Fuerst, Tom. "3 Ways the Church Can Respond to the Capitol Building Riot." *Ministry Matters,* January 13, 2021. https://www.ministrymatters.com/all/entry/10676/3-ways-the-church-can-respond-to-the-capitol-building-riot.

Gerson, Michael. "Faith Requires Us to Be Outraged at Every Violation of Human Dignity." *Deseret,* May 10, 2018. https://www.deseret.com/2018/5/10/20644838/faith-requires-us-to-be-outraged-at-every-violation-of-human-dignity.

Gomes, Peter J. *The Scandalous Gospel of Jesus: What's So Good about the Good News?* San Francisco: HarperOne, 2008.

Gulley, Philip. *Unlearning God: How Unbelieving Helped Me Believe.* New York: Convergent Books, 2018.

Hemingway, Ernest. *A Farewell to Arms.* New York: Charles Scribner's Sons, 1929.

Ipsos Poll. Public Religion Research Institute, as quoted in "QAnon Infects the Church" by Mike Allen.

Jackson, Jesse T. "This Is Not What I Signed Up For." *ChurchLeaders.com,* May 7, 2021. https://churchleaders.com/news/396413-reports-of-an-unsettling-trend-of-pastors-leaving-the-ministry.html.

James, William. *The Varieties of Religious Experience: A Study in Human Nature.* New York: Modern Library, 1902.

Johnson, Samuel. *The Rambler, Number 55*. Charleson, South Carolina: Nabu Press, 2012.

Jones, Robert P. *White Too Long: The Legacy of White Supremacy in American Christianity*. New York: Simon and Schuster, 2020.

Kazantzakis, Nikos. *Zorba the Greek*. New York: Simon and Schuster, 1953.

Keck, L. Robert. *Sacred Eyes*. Synergy Associates, 1993.

Keen, Sam. *To a Dancing God*. New York: Harper and Row, 1970.

Keen, Sam. "What You Ask Is Who You Are." *Spirituality and Health*, May 1, 2000.

Kelly, Thomas R. *A Testament of Devotion*. New York: Harper and Brothers, 1941.

Kushner, Harold S. *How Good Do We Have to Be? A New Understanding of Guilt and Forgiveness*. New York: Back Bay Books, 1996.

Lamott, Anne. Facebook page, January 2022. www.facebook.com/Anne Lamott.

Lomenick, Brad. "Leadership Identity: Part Three." https://leadershiper.lifeway.com.

L'Engle, Madeleine. <www.guideposts.org>.

Mayo Clinic. "Job burnout: How to spot it and take action." June 5, 2021. www.mayoclinic.org.

McSwain, Steve. "Why Nobody Wants to Go to Church Anymore." *Beliefnet*, August 16, 2021.

Medecins Sans Frontiers. "MSF's response to Covid-19 in the United States." April 17, 2020. https://www.doctorswithoutborders.org/latest/faq-msfs-covid-19-response-united-states.

Merton, Thomas. *Love and Living*. Edited by Naomi Burton Stone and Brother Patrick Hart. New York: Bantam Books, 1979.

Mother Teresa. "Reflections on Working Toward Peace." *Architects of Peace*. Santa Clara: Santa Clara University.

Mount, Meher. "Thank You For All The Joy And Pain In My Life." Meher Mount Corporation, October 28, 2015. https://www.mehermount.org/story-blog/2015/10/2810/tthankful-for-suffering..

Muggeridge, Malcolm. *A Twentieth Century Testimony*. Nashville: Thomas Nelson, 1978.

National Public Radio Report, *Morning Edition*. Uroda, Kristen. "If You Feel Thankful, Write It Down. It's Good For Your Health." December 24, 2018.

Newby, James R. *Gathering the Seekers: Spiritual Growth Through Small Group Ministry*. New York: The Alban Institute, 1995.

Newby, James R. *Reflections from the Inner Light: A Journal of Quaker Spirituality*. Eugene: Wipf and Stock Publishers, 2019.

Newby, James R. *Shining Out and Shining In: Understanding the Life Journey of Tom Tipton*. Bloomington: AuthorHouse, 2013.

Newby, James R. and Elizabeth S. Newby. *Between Peril and Promise*. Nashville: Thomas Nelson Publishers, 1984.

Nouwen, Henri J. M. *The Wounded Healer: Ministry in Contemporary Society*. New York: Doubleday Image Books, 1979.

Oliver, Mary. "Of The Empire." In *Dream Work*. New York: Grove, 2010.

Pascal, Blaise. *Pensées*. Translated by A. J. Krailsheimer. New York: Penguin Classics, 1995.

Pasternak, Boris. *Doctor Zhivago*. Italy: Pantheon, 1957.

Pastoral Care, Inc. "Statistics in the Minstry," 2020. https://pastoralcareinc.com/statistics.

Patterson, Stephen J. *The God of Jesus: The Historical Jesus and the Search for Meaning*. Harrisburg: Trinity Press International, 1998.

Patton, Kimberley C. "When the Wounded Emerge as Healers." Cambridge: *Harvard Divinity Bulletin*, Winter 2006.

Peck, M. Scott. *A World Waiting to Be Born: Civility Rediscovered*. New York: Bantam Books, 1993.

Pew Research Center. "Why America's 'nones' don't identify with a religion." August 8, 2018.

Pew Research Center. "Why America's 'nones' left religion behind." August 24, 2016.

Pittenger, Norman. *Alfred North Whitehead*. Cambridge: Lutterworth Press, 1967.

Price, Reynolds. *A Whole New Life: An Illness and a Healing*. New York: Scribner, 2000.

Quindlen, Anna. "Life of the Closed Mind." *Newsweek*, May 29, 2005.

Rohr, Richard. Daily meditation, October 17, 2018.

Rohr, Richard. Facebook page, February 17, 2022. www.facebook.com/David Wheeler.

Rudy. Released October 13, 1993 by TriStar Pictures. Written by Angelo Pizzo and Directed by David Anspaugh.

Saint-Exupéry, Antoine de. *The Little Prince*. Translated by Alan Wakeman. Herefordshire: Wordsworth Classics, 1995.

Shores, Larry. "Richard P. Newby." *Star*, December 15, 1985.

Sinek, Simon. *Start with Why*. New York: Portfolio Penguin Random House. 2011.

Spears, Larry C. "Character and Servant Leadership: Ten Characteristics of Effective, Caring Leaders." *Journal of Virtues and Leadership* 1, no. 1 (2010).

Steinbeck, John. *Travels with Charley: In Search of America*. New York: Viking Penguin, 1962.

Taylor, Barbara Brown. *Leaving Church: A Memoir of Faith*. San Francisco: HarperSanFrancisco, 2006.

Thurman, Howard. *Meditations of the Heart*. Boston: Beacon Press, 1999.

Wilkerson, Isabel. *Caste: The Origins of Our Discontents*. New York: Random House, 2020.

Will, George F. "The Oddness of Everything." *Newsweek*, May 22, 2005.

Wilson, Woodrow. Words above his crypt in the Washington National Cathedral in Washington, D.C.

Woodruff, Paul. *Reverence: Renewing a Forgotten Virtue*. Oxford: Oxford University Press, 2014.

Woolman, John. *The Journal and Major Essays of John Woolman*. Edited by Amelia Gummere. New York: Macmillan, 1992.

Wright, N. T. *God and the Pandemic: A Christian Reflection on the Coronavirus and Its Aftermath*. Grand Rapids: Zondervan, 2020.

~

What Some Participants Have Said about the *Sacred Chaos* Seminar . . .

The small groups and the intimate, laid-back setting were very helpful.

—A Presbyterian Minister

My expectations were more than met! This seminar felt like a rope thrown to a drowning person. I will be forever grateful.

—A United Methodist Minister

I was ready for this seminar. . . . The unhurried pace and the beautiful setting were perfect!

—A Disciples of Christ Minister

I am truly overwhelmed by the degree to which my hopes were exceeded in the Sacred Chaos *seminar. I am very, very grateful and deeply and gently and abundantly blessed. . . . I admire the leadership of this event for the gentle, wise, and spiritual way of encouraging the group as a healing community.*

—A United Methodist Minister

The Sacred Chaos *seminar moved me to a level of trust and sharing which I have not reached with any previous short-term group. . . . The environment fostered was loving, trusting, and, most important, safe. Both of the leaders were very present all the time and came across as being on the journey with us, and not just directing us along. . . . Their compassionate concern for the needs of everyone in the room, the trusting community that was built in just a few short hours, the mutual encouragement to "fear not," and the commitment to staying in touch made this event much more healing and empowering than I could have possibly imagined.*

—A United Methodist Minister

Sacred Chaos was a turning point in my ministry.

—A Presbyterian Minister

Sacred Chaos was a gift of pure grace, a little island of peace where I felt myself being called out of the tomb like Lazarus.

—A United Methodist Minister

For more information about the Sacred Chaos Seminars and this book, please visit the website <https:www.findingyourselfinchaos.org>

Index

About the Authors

Dr. James R. (Jim) Newby is the minister and public friend at Cincinnati Friends (Quaker) Meeting in Cincinnati, Ohio. Before coming to Cincinnati, Jim was the senior minister at the Church of the Savior in Oklahoma City, Oklahoma; the minister of faith and learning at Wayzata Community Church in Wayzata, Minnesota; and the minister of spiritual growth at Plymouth Congregational Church in Des Moines, Iowa. He has served as the executive director of the Yokefellow Institute at Earlham College in Richmond, Indiana, and was on the faculty of the Earlham School of Religion. Jim holds degrees from Friends University, Earlham School of Religion, William Penn University, and Princeton Theological Seminary. He is the author and editor of eleven books, including *Gathering the Seekers* (Alban Institute), *Sacred Chaos: One Man's Spiritual Journey through Pain and Loss* (Continuum), and *Reflections from the Inner Light: A Journal of Quaker Spirituality* (Wipf and Stock).

Dr. Mark Minear earned his PhD in counseling psychology from Ball State University in 1997. He returned to graduate school after twenty years in the pastoral ministry. Besides Ball State, he holds degrees from the Earlham School of Religion and William Penn University. He is currently a licensed psychologist in the state of Iowa and practices full-time, providing psychotherapy, assessment, consultation, and training. Mark utilizes a multidimensional model of wellness in his therapeutic approach; this allows for his clients to work across physical, emotional, intellectual, vocational, social, environmental, and spiritual domains. He is on the team of counselors at the Des Moines Pastoral Counseling Center.